Small Home Plans

Edited by Garlinghouse

Small
Home
Plans

Edited by Garlinghouse

THE GARLINGHOUSE COMPANY
Topeka, Kansas

SMALL HOME PLANS

A Garlinghouse Company publication.

ISBN 0-938708-04-X

Printed in the United States of America.

Library of Congress catalog card number 82-81518.

Small Home Plans

Value and elegance combined

No. 25016—This design uses rough-finished wood on both exterior and interior walls, which saves labor and reduces maintenance later on. Tongue-and-groove decking over exposed joists substitutes for expensive floors and ceilings. The plan packs seven rooms, two baths, a dressing area, and a mud room into just two of the three floors. The lowest level, not shown, could easily be finished later. Floor-to-ceiling glass in the two-story living room produces a feeling of openness to the outside.

Main level—990 sq. ft.
Upper level—565 sq. ft.
Basement—900 sq. ft.

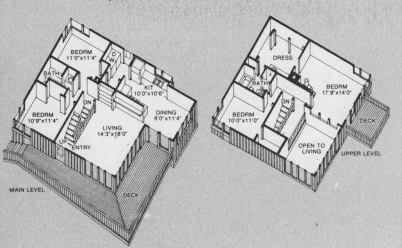

Contemporary ranch design

No. 26740—Sloping cathedral ceilings are found throughout the entirety of this home. A kitchen holds the central spot in the floor plan. It is partially open to a great hall with firebox and deck access on one side, daylight room lit by ceiling glass and full length windows on another, and entryway hallway on a third. The daylight room leads out onto a unique double deck. Bedrooms lie to the outside of the plan. Two smaller bedrooms at the rear share a full bath. The more secluded master bedroom at the front has its own full bath and access to a private deck. A double garage completes the design. Crawl space construction is detailed.

Living area—1,512 sq. ft.
Garage—478 sq. ft.

Photos courtesy:
The American Wood Council
Washington, D.C.

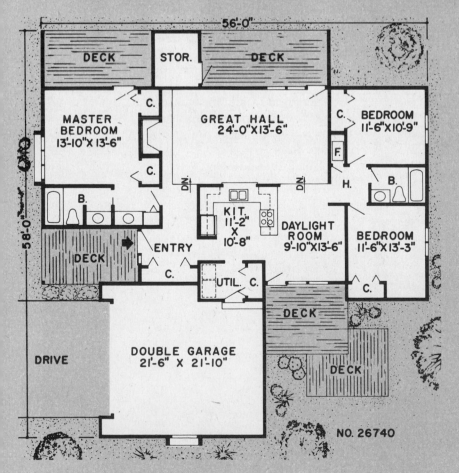

56'-0"

DECK	STOR.	DECK	

MASTER
BEDROOM
13'-10" X 13'-6"

C.

C.

GREAT HALL
24'-0"X13'-6"

C.

BEDROOM
11'-6"X10'-9"

F.

58'-0"

B.

DN.

DN.

H.

B.

KIT.
11'-2"
X
10'-8"

DAYLIGHT
ROOM
9'-10"X13'-6"

BEDROOM
11'-6"X13'-3"

ENTRY

C.

UTIL.

C.

C.

DECK

DECK

DECK

DRIVE

DOUBLE GARAGE
21'-6" X 21'-10"

NO. 26740

Country living

No. 26860—The design of this comfortable home says country living at its best. Constructed of energy-efficient wood for beauty and warmth, this home offers room for a growing family at an affordable price. The master bedroom and bath are on the second floor with a small deck. Two bedrooms and a bath are separated from the living area on the main level by the foyer. The living room and family room both have their own deck. A large eat-in kitchen and separate dining room complete this energy conscious design.

First floor—1,434 sq. ft.
Second floor—369 sq. ft.

Photos courtesy:
The American Wood Council
Washington, D.C.

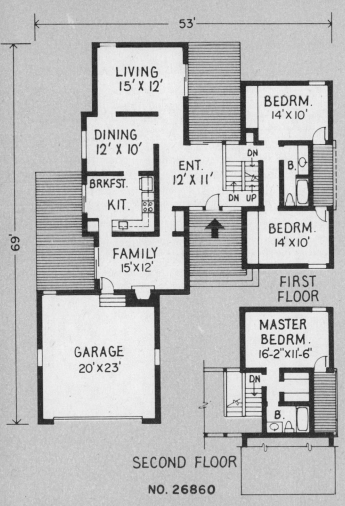

LIVING
15' X 12'

DINING
12' X 10'

BRKFST.

KIT.

FAMILY
15' X 12'

GARAGE
20' X 23'

ENT.
12' X 11'

DN

DN UP

BEDRM.
14' X 10'

B.

BEDRM.
14' X 10'

FIRST FLOOR

53'

69'

MASTER
BEDRM.
16'-2" X 11'-6"

DN

B.

SECOND FLOOR

NO. 26860

Prize winner

No. 19863—This cozy solar house took top prize in a nationwide design contest. Inside is a floor plan that's flexible enough to satisfy a wide variety of families and life-styles. The dominant feature of this passive solar system is the 32-foot-long greenhouse where the sun's heat is collected, stored and shared with the rest of the house, cutting energy bills in half. The house offers open spaces and partial ceilings to maximize airflow throughout.

First floor—1,000 sq. ft.
Second floor—572 sq. ft.
Greenhouse—272 sq. ft.

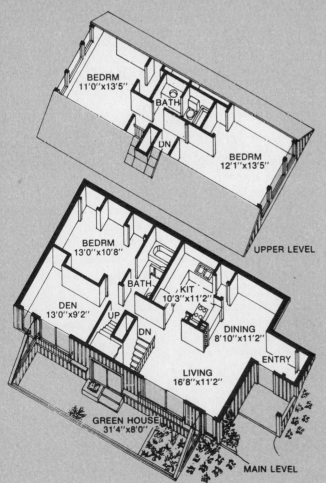

BEDRM
11'0"x13'5"

BATH

DN

BEDRM
12'1"x13'5"

UPPER LEVEL

BEDRM
13'0"x10'8"

BATH

KIT
10'3"x11'2"

DEN
13'0"x9'2"

UP

DN

DINING
8'10"x11'2"

ENTRY

LIVING
16'8"x11'2"

GREEN HOUSE
31'4"x8'0"

MAIN LEVEL

Unique passive solar system utilized

No. 26090—This home was designed specifically for use with the One Design Waterwall passive solar system across its southern side. Mounted easily between studs like insulation, it is then filled with tap water and the sun does the rest. Decorating possibilities are endless. Other solar features include a northern trombe wall heated by the sun's rays through clerestory windows, an air-lock entry and concrete slab floor construction. Exterior walls show 2x6 studs with R-19 insulation. The floor plan features an L-shaped great room living area, three bedrooms and one and a half baths. The kitchen is very open and details an angled island sink area with built-in dishwasher.

Living area—1,258 sq. ft.
Storage—30 sq. ft.

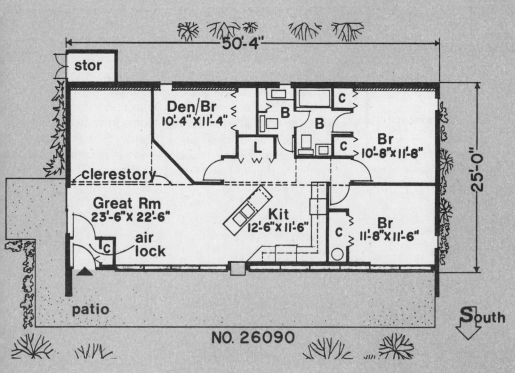

50'-4"

stor

Den/Br
10'-4" x 11'-4"

B

B

C

C

Br
10'-8" x 11'-8"

L

C

clerestory

Great Rm
23'-6" x 22'-6"

Kit
12'-6" x 11'-6"

C

Br
11'-8" x 11'-6"

air
lock

C

25'-0"

patio

South

NO. 26090

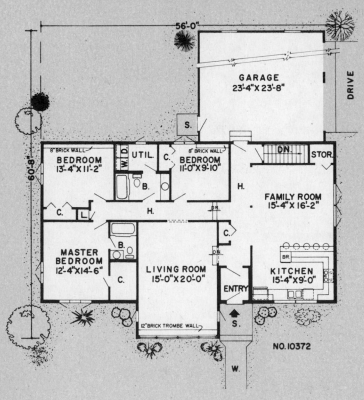

Active/passive combination

10372—The exterior appearance of this house readily draws your attention to its passive and active solar systems. Features include large triple glazed south windows, solar roof panels and a trombe thermal wall which receives heat gain from the sun to radiate into the room on cloudy days or at night. Heat gain is also obtained from clerestory windows which shed the sun's rays on solid brick north walls. A six inch concrete floor is employed for heat gain and storage. An open family room forms the focus of the floor plan. A formal living room, three bedrooms, two baths and a utility room are more secluded. The family room flows into the bright south-facing kitchen through a dining bar window. A double garage sits at the rear and is reached through a side entrance. Varied roof pitches give height to the single-level design.

Living area—1,787 sq. ft.
Basement—650 sq. ft.
Garage—576 sq. ft.

Studio loft offers versatility to passive plan

No. 10388—Sunwall water tubes and clay tile floors gather and store solar heat generated during the day through many southern glass doors, windows and skylights. Located on the lower level are a more formal living room with wood stove, kitchen area which extends through an eating bar to the family room, two bedrooms and two full baths. Laundry facilities are tucked into the master bedroom bath area. The second unfolds into a large storage area which also houses the hot water heater and furnace, and studio loft with its own private deck. Closet space is ample here. Northern skylights add their illumination. The loft overlooks the family room from a balcony. This openness of design allows for maximum air circulation. A double garage, plentious in storage, concludes the plan.

First floor—1,248 sq. ft.
Studio loft—357 sq. ft.
Garage—640 sq. ft.

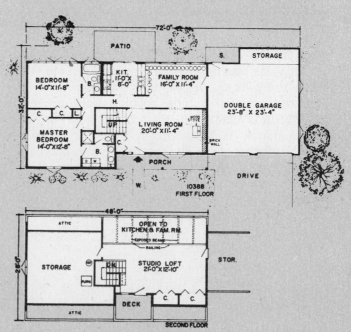

11

Modified version of this design with roll doors closed . . .   and roll doors open.

French country charmer

No. 25040—Practical because it's made of low-maintenance materials such as grooved plywood siding below and hand-split cedar roof shakes above. In addition, the central utility core cuts construction costs as does the bold mansard roof which also forms the walls of the upper level. The second floor exterior walls slope in approximately two feet from the floor to the ceiling. The covered carport protects the main entrance and doubles as a sheltered play area for children. A small outdoor storage unit, 12'x4' with sliding doors for access, is modeled after the house.

Main level—864 sq. ft.
Upper level—864 sq. ft.

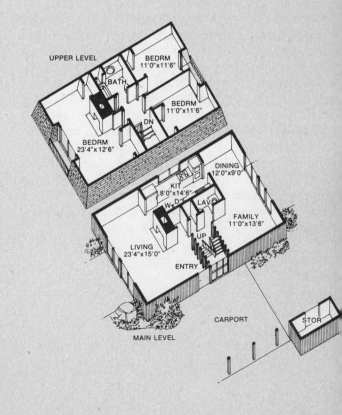

Energy requirements reduced by passive solar plan

No. 26091—The One Design Waterwall passive solar system is only one energy efficient detail of this design. The waterwalls, which cover the entire front of the home, mount easily between studs and go to work when filled with tap water. Vinyl-sided roll doors cover the waterwalls on the outside when not in use. An air lock entry, concrete slab construction, and living room fireplace further reduce energy needs. Three bedrooms are zoned to the right as you enter. A large living room/dining area lies to the left. Efficiently arranged between the two zones and at the rear are a bath, kitchen, laundry area. The washer and dryer are hidden behind bi-fold doors in the kitchen and linen shelves are tucked around the corner in the hall. A single car garage finishes the plan.

Living area—1,215 sq. ft.
Garage—283 sq. ft.

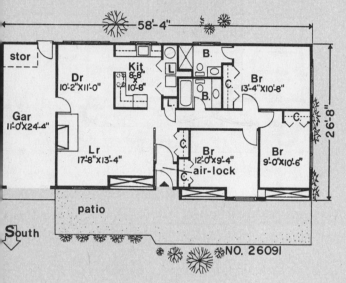

Distinctive living . . .

No. 8266—An attractive exterior with a most convenient and livable interior. There are three large bedrooms with two full baths. You will enjoy the living room with the interior wall fireplace. The modern built-in kitchen is flanked to the left by the dining room and on the right by a dinette. Note the sliding and folding doors between the kitchen, the dining room and living room. The stairway marked DN leads to the basement which provides more utility space as well as future recreational areas.

**First floor—1,604 sq. ft., Garage—455 sq. ft.
Basement—1,604 sq. ft.**

Screened porch designed for dining

No. 8262—Opening to dining room and convenient to kitchen, the screened porch extends this stone veneer plan and offers sheltered open air dining. Placing the fireplace in the corner of the living room succeeds in spreading the atmosphere over the entire living-dining area, and unique expanses of windows flood the areas with light. Master bedroom merits full bath with shower.

**First floor—1,406 sq. ft., Basement—1,394 sq. ft.
Garage—444 sq. ft.**

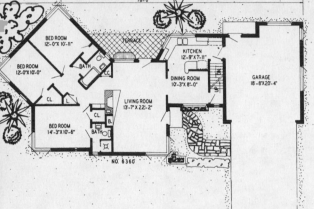

Ranch style favors living room

No. 6360—Stretching over 22 feet to span the width of this ranch design, the living room is indulged with expanses of windows, wood-burning fireplace, and access to the terrace. Separate, well-windowed dining room and efficient kitchen with abundant counter space border the living room.

House—1,293 sq. ft., Basement—767 sq. ft.
Garage—466 sq. ft., Terract—92 sq. ft.

A Cape Cod beauty

No. 9068—This beautiful Cape Cod home will fit into any up-to-date community. Note the compactness of the plan and how every inch of space is used to good advantage. There are no costly offsets in the plan and the rooms on the second floor have been made habitable by the addition of dormers, resulting in minimum construction costs. The exterior walls are frame, brick veneered. Plans show a full basement.

First floor—1,090 sq. ft., Second floor—652 sq. ft.
Basement—1,090 sq. ft.

Open and airy

No. 7138—This contemporary split-level for modern Americans has studio ceilings with exposed beams and a tiled entryway. You will enjoy the light airy country kitchen with built-ins and a breakfast bar. There is a planter near by and sliding glass doors leading to the terrace. Three bedrooms with large bath on upper level as well as a sun deck for your enjoyment. Ample storage, laundry and utility space in the lower level with 11' by 13' den and full shower bath.

Upper level—1,291 sq. ft., Lower level-1,446 sq. ft.
Garage—459 sq. ft., Basement—683 sq. ft.

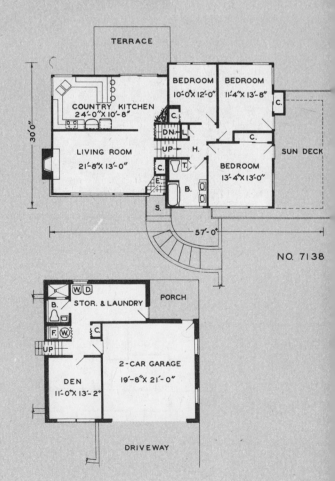

Move in today — finish it later

No. 9115—This unusual but quite attractive story and one-half home features a spiral stairway to the second floor. An alternate is shown for those that prefer a more conventional stairway. The three bedrooms on the upper level could be left unfinished by the contractor and then finished by the man of the house during his leisure hours. The family room would serve as the master bedroom in this case. The kitchen area is quite nice with an abundance of cabinets, a separate laundry and a large breakfast nook.

First floor—1,185 sq. ft., Second floor—549 sq. ft. Garage—484 sq. ft.

*For price and order information
see pages 108-109*

NO. 9115

TERRACE

SPIRAL STAIRWAY

ALTERNATE STAIRWAY

L. HALL
DN

EQUIP. RM.
HALL
LAU.
D.W.
FAMILY ROOM
18'-0" X 13'-8"
KITCHEN
10'-0" X 11'-0"

DOUBLE GARAGE
21'-4" X 20'-4"
B.
C. L. C.
HALL
BREAKFAST AREA
10'-0"X7'-2"
UP
LIVING ROOM
18'-0" X 14'-6"
DINING
10'-4" X 10'-0"

APRON
P.
W.

ALTERNATE STAIRWAY
HALL
UP
C. STOR
DRIVE
LOWER LEVEL
61'-0"
LOWER LEVEL

MASTER BEDROOM
17'-8" X 10'-8"
B.
C. C.
H.
BEDROOM
11'-4" X 10'-0"
36'-0"
BEDROOM
16'-4" X 10'-6"
C.

UPPER LEVEL
UPPER LEVEL

One-story links dignity, luxury

No. 9390—Stately arches and simple brick create a facade that expresses Spanish-flavored dignity; inside, the floor plan succeeds in fusing luxury and convenience. Located at rear, the double garage provides convenience in transporting groceries, yet does not detract from the lines of the home. Entry is via the closeted foyer and hallway, which efficiently separate living and sleeping areas, with an elongated living room at night. The bodering kitchen and dining room are well-planned and include space for washer and dryer as well as small patio reached through sliding glass doors.

First floor—1,660 sq. ft., Garage—535 sq. ft.

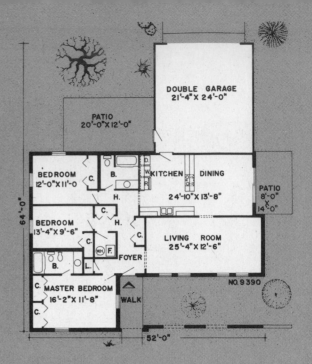

Arches, iron work grace one-story plan

No. 9386—Brick arches, exposed beams, and intriguing grillwork create a one-story home with a Spanish accent; inside, the floor plan maximizes the single level advantages. The elongated kitchen/dining area can choose informality or partition to form a separate dining room, while the adjoining laundry center is well located to save steps. Served by two full baths, each of the three bedrooms is comfortably large and equipped with adequate closet space. Living and family rooms furnish activity areas.

First floor—1,695 sq. ft., Garage—585 sq. ft.

*For price and order information
see pages 108-109*

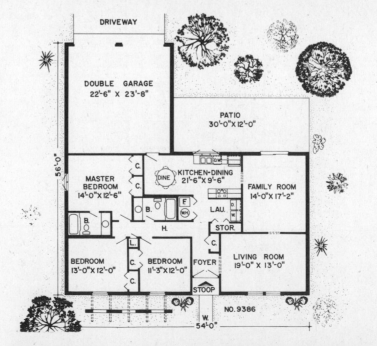

Basement—Great for indoor, outdoor living

No. 9368—The Spanish influence of this ranch home provides character that will be an asset to any community. The floor plan is quite practical and is conveniently arranged. There are two large bathrooms, an excellent traffic pattern, and a well-designed kitchen. The garage is extra large and has the entrance at the rear. The garage door can be installed in front if necessary.

First floor—1,587 sq. ft., Basement—1,587 sq. ft. Garage— 490 sq. ft.

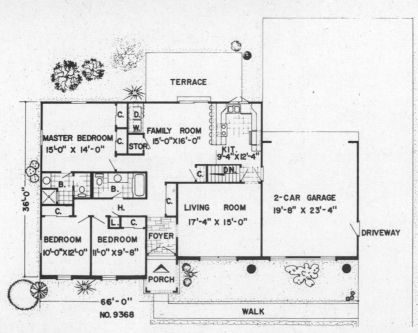

TERRACE

MASTER BEDROOM
15'-0" X 14'-0"

C. D.
W.
C. STOR.

FAMILY ROOM
15'-0"X16'-0"

KIT.
9'-4"X12'-4"

C.
DN.

B.
B.

C.
H.

36'-0"

BEDROOM
10'-0"X12'-0"

BEDROOM
11'-0"X9'-8"

L. C.

FOYER

C.

LIVING ROOM
17'-4" X 15'-0"

2-CAR GARAGE
19'-8" X 23'-4"

DRIVEWAY

PORCH

66'-0"

NO. 9368

WALK

Compact floor plan benefits traditional

No. 9366—Space-saving and highly functional, this attractive one-story traditional incorporates three bedrooms and a detailed kitchen/dining area, all within 1,400 square feet. Bedrooms are roomy and well-closeted, and two full baths are provided. Located off the foyer, the living room promises both a quiet nook for conversation and easy access to all areas of the home. Sliding glass doors separate the patio from the kitchen/dining area, which involves a pantry, laundry niche and garage entrance.

First floor—1,400 sq. ft., Basement—1,408 sq. ft. Garage—493 sq. ft.

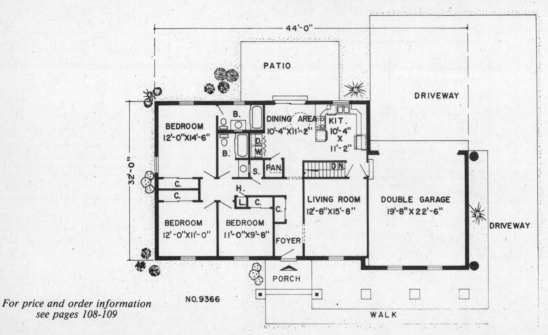

For price and order information see pages 108-109

NO. 9366

Spanish accents create stately facade

No. 9394—Gracefully arched windows and doorways and an unusual chimney treatment are among the ornate touches that lend this single level plan its Spanish charm. Accessible from the gracious foyer, the elongated living room provides a substantial area for entertaining guests. Bordering the living room is a formal dining room. A family/dining area serves to focus family activities. Three bedrooms, each with plentiful closet space, and two full baths are shown.

First floor—1,628 sq. ft., Garage—633 sq. ft.

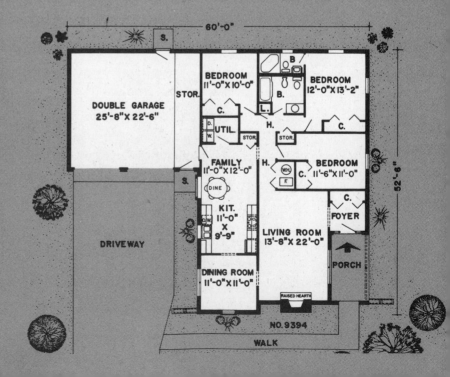

NO. 9394

20

Contemporary has many desirable features

No. 9344—This beautiful contemporary home has many desirable features. There are three bedrooms and two full baths. The master bedroom has over 13 feet of closet space. It also has sliding glass doors which open onto the terrace. The family room also has sliding glass doors. The kitchen is compact but very efficient and includes the washer, dryer and eating space. The garage has a large storage area at the rear.

First floor—1,496 sq. ft., Basement—1,496 sq. ft. Garage—480 sq. ft.

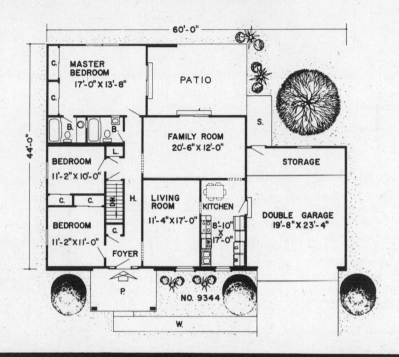

Country flavor colors interior

No. 146—Generously proportioned rooms and an immense country kitchen with breakfast bar and barbecue oven sketch a portrait of quaint and cozy charm within this brick-trimmed ranch. Bordered by the rear terrace, the kitchen is fully as large as the lavish living room and will undoubtedly rival the living room as a haven for informal gatherings. The compartmented bath is also distinctive and annexes the master bedroom's powder room to form an elongated and practical complex.

**First floor—1,296 sq. ft., Basement—1,296 sq. ft.
Garage and storage—477 sq. ft.**

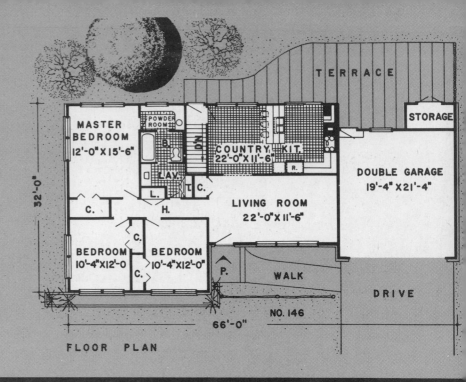

Fireplace breathes life into room

No. 9296—Laced with intriguing diamond light windows, the living room of this well-proportioned plan catches light and life from the wood-burning fireplace. The informal family room merits sliding glass doors which open to the terrace and borders the kitchen with breakfast bar, laundry area, and pantry. Closet space is generously sprinkled throughout the house, especially in the master bedroom. Double sinks benefit the hall bath which serves two more bedrooms.

**First floor—1,522 sq. ft., Basement—1,522 sq. ft.
Garage—470 sq. ft.**

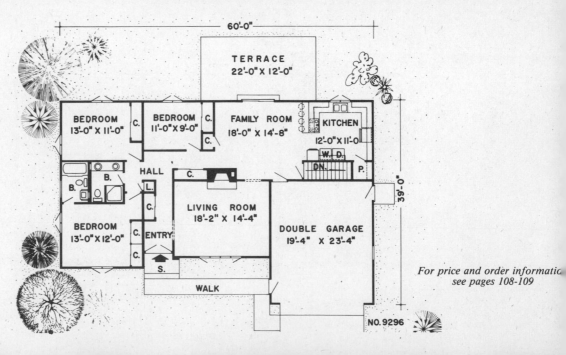

*For price and order information
see pages 108-109*

22

Bedroom doubles as den

No. 9233—This small but quite attractive brick veneer home contains a minimum amount of waste space. The floor plan is arranged to provide maximum convenience. The basement contains a bath room with a shower. The exterior is unusually attractive for a home containing less than 1200 square feet.

First floor—1,190 sq. ft., Basement—1,190 sq. ft. Carport—416 sq. ft.

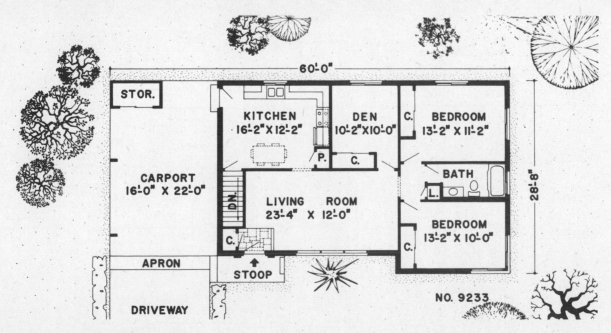

Handy workshop edges double garage

No. 324—Spanning over 19 feet, the workshop fringing the garage provides a perfect hobby area and offers access to rear yard and kitchen-dining area. Filling 1475 square feet of living area, this double-garaged ranch style boasts three sizable bedrooms plus a den. Two tiled baths, one with double sinks, serve the sleeping quarters, and the living room adjoins the den, suggesting its use as television room or family room. Generous space is allotted the kitchen, open to the dining room via breakfast bar, and a tiled entrance foyer will prove useful in channeling traffic.

First floor—1,475 sq. ft., Basement—1,475 sq. ft. Garage—512 sq. ft.

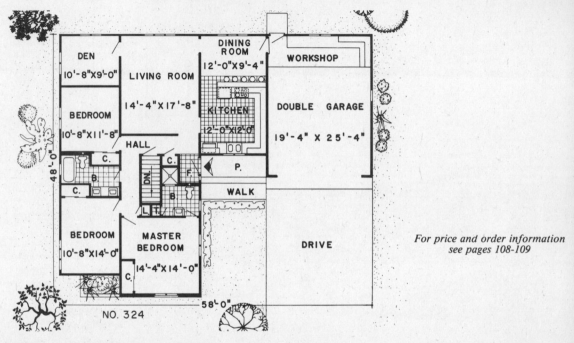

DEN
10'-8"X9'-0"

LIVING ROOM
14'-4"X17'-8"

BEDROOM
10'-8"X11'-8"

HALL

BEDROOM
10'-8"X14'-0"

MASTER BEDROOM
14'-4"X14'-0"

DINING ROOM
12'-0"X9'-4"

KITCHEN
12'-0"X12'-0"

WORKSHOP

DOUBLE GARAGE
19'-4" X 25'-4"

P.

WALK

DRIVE

48'-0"

58'-0"

NO. 324

For price and order information see pages 108-109

Painted brick splashes spacious design

No. 306—Three bedrooms and plenty of living space are encased in this contemporary plan, highlighted on the exterior by contrasting painted brick and vertical siding. Two baths, one private to the master bedroom, fill the sleeping area to the right of the foyer. L-shaped living-dining room contributes formality and connects to the kitchen via folding door. For relaxed living, the family room opens to the terrace through sliding glass doors. Laundry and storage space benefit the functional kitchen.

First floor—1,581 sq. ft. Carport and storage—537 sq. ft.

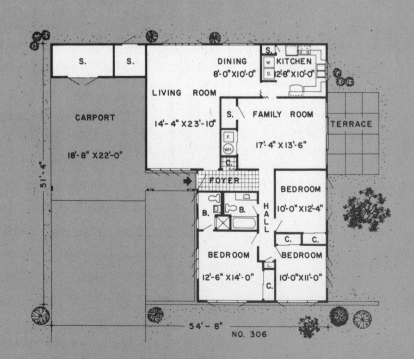

S.   S.

CARPORT
18'-8" X 22'-0"

DINING
8'-0"X10'-0"

KITCHEN
12'-8"X10'-0"

LIVING ROOM
14'-4" X 23'-10"

FAMILY ROOM
17'-4" X 13'-6"

TERRACE

FOYER

HALL

BEDROOM
10'-0"X12'-4"

BEDROOM
12'-6" X14'-0"

BEDROOM
10'-0"X11'-0"

51'-4"

54'-8"

NO. 306

24

Concrete block conceives unusual facade

No. 296—Concrete block veneer is artfully blended with battened and vertical siding to achieve a striking effect in this moderate size contemporary. Carport and terrace wing the basic rectangular design while retaining its economy. Living and dining rooms equally savor the wood-burning fireplace, and sliding glass doors open the area to the outdoors. Three bedrooms, two baths, and bountiful storage space comprise the sleeping area, and additional storage closets line the carport.

First floor—1,351 sq. ft.
Carport and storage—484 sq. ft.

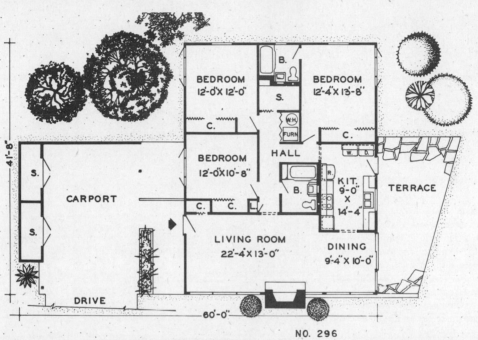

BEDROOM 12'-0" X 12'-0"

B.

S.

BEDROOM 12'-4" X 13'-8"

C.

W.H. FURN

C.

W. D.

BEDROOM 12'-0" X 10'-8"

HALL

CARPORT

S.

S.

B.

R.

KIT. 9'-0" X 14'-4"

TERRACE

C.

C.

LIVING ROOM 22'-4" X 13'-0"

DINING 9'-4" X 10'-0"

41'-8"

DRIVE

60'-0"

NO. 296

Distinctive carport has many uses

No. 9786—The carport between this home and its garage can be enclosed to form a den or separate family room, can be used as roofed patio or play area, or can be screened to provide comfortable outdoor dining. The foyer directs traffic to the three bedrooms, the living room or the family kitchen. This deluxe kitchen not only has a breakfast bar and space for dining, but room for washer and dryer as well. The living room opens onto an attractive stone terrace.

**First floor—1,391 sq. ft., Carport—288 sq. ft.
Garage—336 sq. ft.**

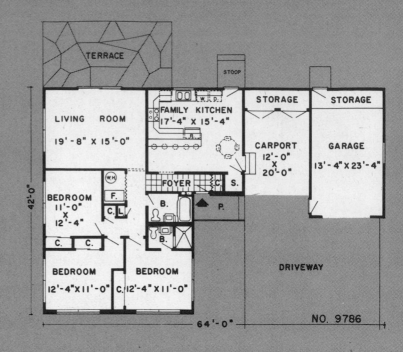

Fireplace a feature

No. 9838—Family convenience is emphasized in this beautiful Ranch style home. The owner's suite includes double closets and a private bath with a spacious built-in vanity. A two-way wood burning fireplace between the living room and dining room permits the fire to be enjoyed from both rooms. An extra large garage possesses an abundance of extra storage space.

**First floor—1,770 sq. ft., Basement—1,770 sq. ft.
Garage—700 sq. ft.**

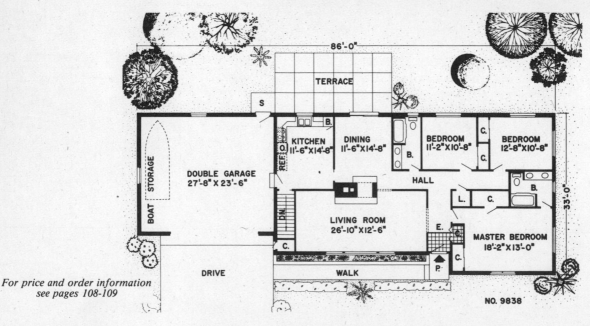

*For price and order information
see pages 108-109*

26

Family living with traditional flair

No. 9824—Outdoor living areas and facilities for entertaining guests were prime requirements when designing this beautiful home. The living room features a wood burning fireplace and sliding glass doors which open onto the large flagstone terrace. Another fireplace and a built-in bar-b-que grill are in the family room. Another built-in bar-b-que grill is located on the terrace. A full basement provides space for indoor recreational activities, such as ping pong, billiards, etc. a well designed centrally located kitchen will delight the busy housewife.

First floor—1,668 sq. ft., Basement—1,668 sq. ft.
Garage—528 sq. ft.

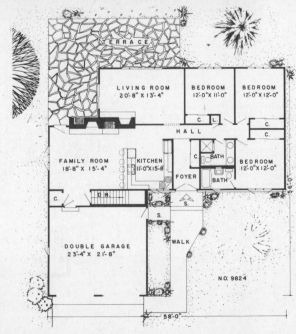

Chimney accents charming cottage

No. 304—Hipped roof and brick chimney embellish this appealing design, perfect for a narrow lot and adaptable to a lakeside or mountain retreat. Inside, the wood-burning fireplace produces a cozy living and dining area, bordered by a highly efficient corridor kitchen. Three bedrooms are nestled in the sleeping area and share a well-placed bath. The smallest bedroom would make an excellent den or nursery, and a separate utility and storage room fringes the kitchen. Coat closet is placed near the entry for convenience.

First floor—888 sq. ft.

*For price and order information
see pages 108-109*

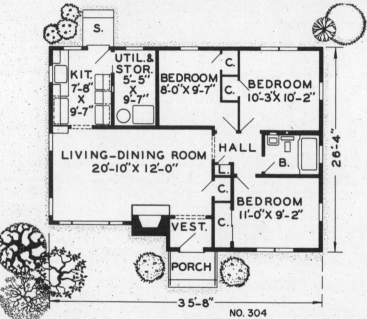

NO. 304

Design offers economy, luxury

No. 292—Condensed to only 1156 square feet, this economy plan features three bedrooms, two full baths, and a floor plan detailed to promote living. Entry is into the living room, with coat closet immediately available, and adjoining dining room is separated for formality. The kitchen complex is efficent and supplies partitioned laundry center and broom closet. Three bedrooms include a master bedroom with full bath and plentiful closet space. Storage is neatly placed behind the carport, and the front porch is roofed and welcome for summer relaxation.

**First floor—1,156 sq. ft., Storage—60 sq. ft.
Carport—220 sq. ft., Porch—100 sq. ft.**

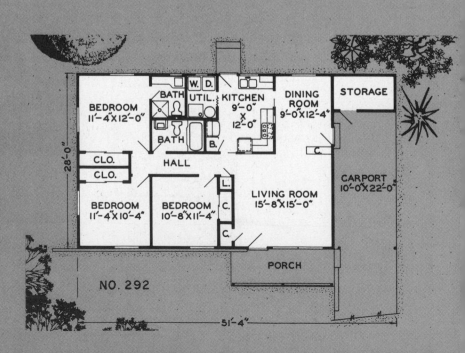

NO. 292

28

Two dining areas serve compact plan

No. 294—Trim and economical, this three bedroom plan offers two separate dining areas, open to kitchen and living room. Hipped roof exterior is decked in brick for ease of maintenance, while the interior is carefully zoned. Three bedrooms fill the sleeping wing, separated from kitchen by folding door. Large, full bath is convenient to both living and sleeping zones, and closet space is adequate. Space for utilities, storage, and recreation is housed in the full basement.

First floor—1,154 sq. ft., Basement—1,154 sq. ft.

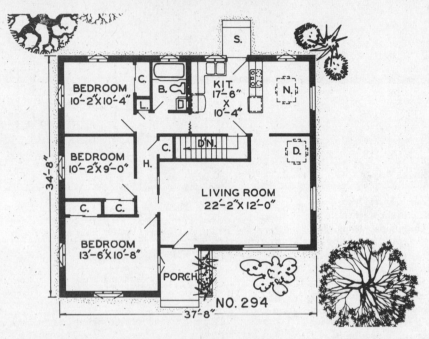

Foyer focus of L-shaped plan

No. 9816—Placed to permit immediate access to all rooms, the closeted foyer helps maintain the fine balance of this stone-trimmed contemporary. Only a few steps from the bedroom hall and formal living room, the foyer steers traffic to the kitchen, basement, or the richly finished family room with fireplace and sliding glass doors to the terrace. The kitchen allots a casual dining area and offers dining service to the terrace as well. Closets are plentiful and a full basement is provided.

**First floor—1,528 sq. ft., Basement—1,232 sq. ft.
Garage—618 sq. ft.**

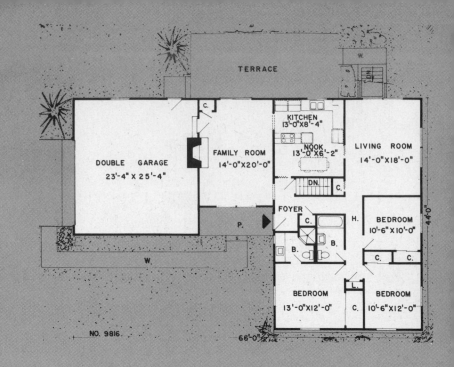

Wood paneling enhances foyer

No. 9712—A tiled entrance foyer with wood paneled walls directs traffic to the kitchen, living room or bedroom area. The compact living space on the first floor is supplemented by a full basement. This country kitchen opens directly to the family room, which has sliding glass doors to a side terrace. A full bath opens off the master bedroom. Two more bedrooms share a bathroom. This extra-sized garage adds storage space. Solar screen block walls shade the house from the sun and provide privacy for the front bedrooms.

**First floor—1,554 sq. ft., Basement—1,554 sq. ft.
Garage—535 sq. ft.**

*For price and order information
see pages 108-109*

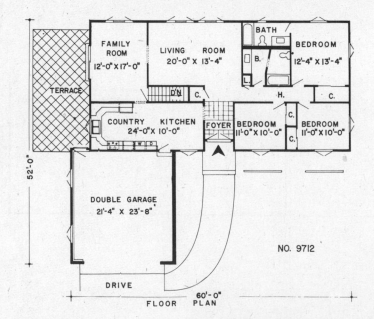

Built-in workbench benefits plan

No. 134—Highly ornamented and layered with brick and diamond light windows, the facade of this rectangular plan envelops an interior that is carefully planned, even to include a built-in workbench. Storage is also planned inside the double garage, which is edged by a kitchen complete with laundry and dining nooks. Sliding glass doors separate flagstone terrace from family room, which supplements the 25-foot living room. Three bedrooms utilize two full baths, and a full basement is outlined.

First floor—1,504 sq. ft., Basement—1,504 sq. ft.
Garage—528 sq. ft.

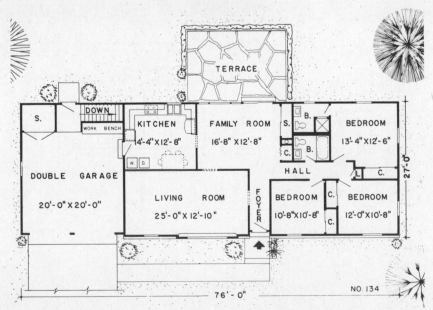

Mud room separates garage, kitchen

No. 9812—Gardening and woodworking tools will find a home in the storage closet of the useful mud room in this rustic detailed ranch. Besides incorporating a laundry area, the mud room will prove invaluable as a place for removing snowy boots and draining wet umbrellas. The family room appendages the open kitchen and flows outward to the stone terrace. The master bedroom is furnished with private bath and protruding closet space, and the living room retains a formality by being situated to the left of the entryway.

First floor—1,396 sq. ft., Basement—1,396 sq. ft. Garage—484 sq. ft.

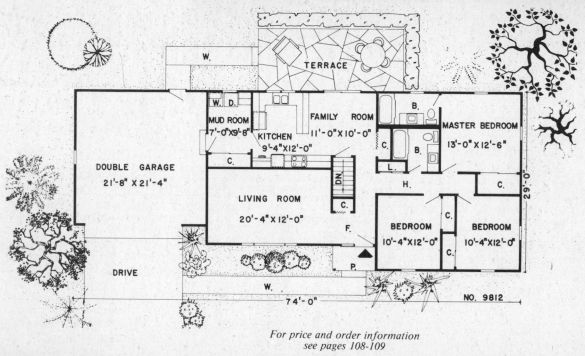

*For price and order information
see pages 108-109*

Design fits all settings

No. 9652—Take this house feature by feature and you will decide that you want to live in it. It has cathedral ceilings throughout the house which provides a feeling of spaciousness. The master bedroom has a dressing area, a private bath and two large closets. The kitchen has easy access to all parts of the house as well as the basement and outdoors. The family room opens onto a colorful flagstone terrace through sliding glass doors.

First floor—1,594 sq. ft., Basement—1,594 sq. ft. Garage—484 sq. ft.

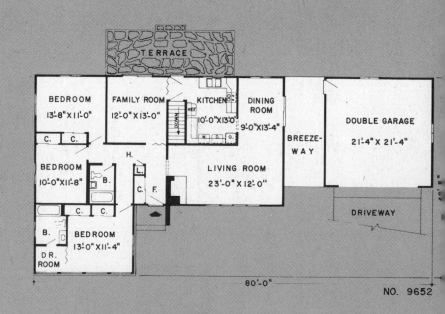

32

Secluded patio, garden and terrace

No. 9586—This house is completely contemporary and offers easy living for the entire family. The master bedroom has access to the covered terrace and also has its own private bath with tiled shower. Sliding glass doors open onto the terrace from the living room. The kitchen and family room open onto a small flagstone patio which serves as an outdoor dining area. The enclosed garden across the front of the house is an unusual but desirable feature. The portico (walkway covering) is both functional and attractive. It helps form a secluded garden retreat and also serves as a covered walkway from the garage to the main entrance.

First floor—1,490 sq. ft., Basement—1,245 sq. ft. Garage—609 sq. ft.

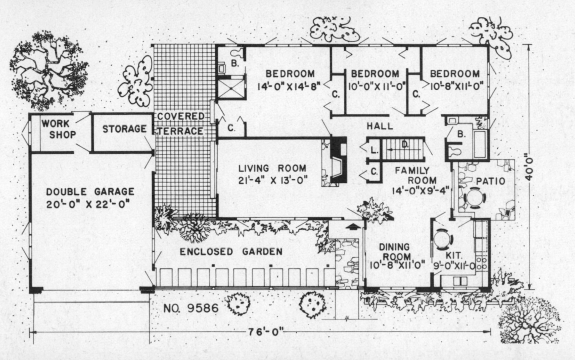

WORK SHOP

STORAGE

COVERED TERRACE

B.

BEDROOM
14'-0" X 14'-8"

BEDROOM
10'-0"X 11'-0"

BEDROOM
10'-8"X11'-0"

C.

C.

HALL

B.

C.

DOUBLE GARAGE
20'-0" X 22'-0"

LIVING ROOM
21'-4" X 13'-0"

L.

D.

C.

FAMILY ROOM
14'-0"X9'-4"

PATIO

40'0"

ENCLOSED GARDEN

DINING ROOM
10'-8"X11'0"

KIT.
9'-0"X12'-0"

NO. 9586

76'-0"

Diamond light windows garnish design

No. 286—Ornamental fascia boards and diamond light windows embroider the exterior of this hardy ranch style and preview the attention to detail within. Closeted entry hall is flanked by formal living room to the right and open family area to the left. The kitchen-family room combination merges work and play areas and includes laundry space. Three bedrooms line the rear and full bath is assigned to the master bedroom. Double garage and storage area are provided.

First floor—1,450 sq. ft., Garage—463 sq. ft.

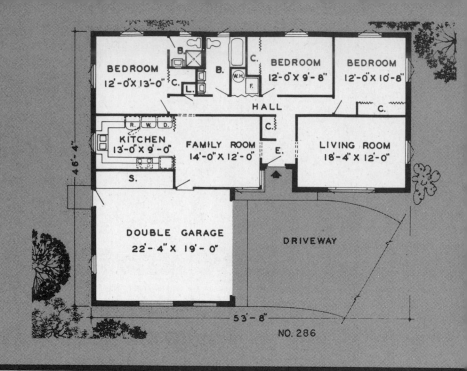

Three bedrooms augment inexpensive plan

No. 295—Conservative and uncluttered inside and out, this three bedroom home affords comfortable living without unreasonable expense. Useful extras, such as a fireplace in the living room, a hall linen closet, and a substantial kitchen with dining area supplement a well-designed interior. The full basement might eventually be finished to accommodate a family room, workshop or child's playroom. Edging the living room and kitchen is a carport bordered by storage area.

First floor—1,040 sq. ft., Basement—1,040 sq. ft. Carport—288 sq. ft., Storage—72 sq. ft.

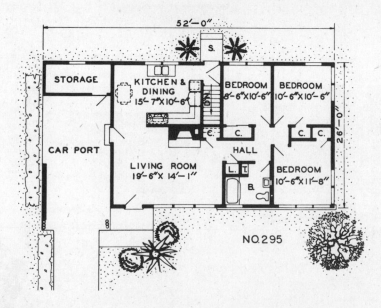

For price and order information see pages 108-109

Comfortable living on a modest budget

No. 282—This very attractive brick veneer house appears much larger than it really is. The house contains only 1,190 square feet. The kitchen and dining room are combined to add spaciousness to these areas. They are separated only by the kitchen cabinets which contain the built-in range and oven. The utility room has space for the washer and dryer as well as the furnace and water heater. Adequate storage area is provided behind the garage. Access to the flagstone terrace is gained through sliding glass doors in the dining room.

First floor—1,190 sq. ft., Garage—450 sq. ft.

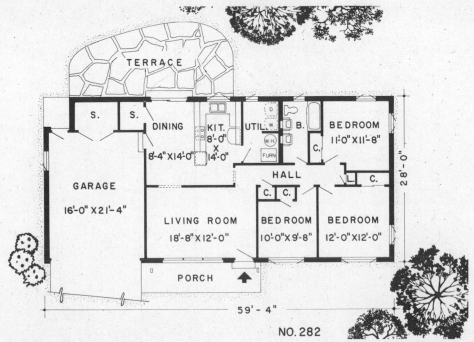

NO. 282

Modest design year round retreat

No. 293—Adaptable to a vacation setting or a suburban lot, this well-proportioned home can be constructed on a moderate budget. The expense-reducing rectangular plan offers two spacious bedrooms plus another smaller bedroom that would make an excellent den, study or television room. A wood-burning fireplace flavors the living room and the home's exterior is garlanded by a stone planting box winging the front entrance porch.

First floor—1,000 sq. ft., Basement—1,000 sq. ft.

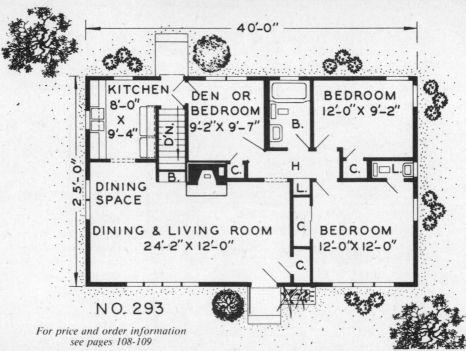

*For price and order information
see pages 108-109*

Cathedral ceilings enhance entire plan

No. 228—This exceptionally attractive front to back split level house is designed for a narrow lot. A perfectly flat lot can be used or a lot that slopes to the rear will work equally well. Cathedral ceilings are used throughout the house adding an air of spaciousness. A large breakfast area is provided in the kitchen. The extra large family room on the lower level is well lighted by casement type windows above the grade line. Glass doors in the dining room open onto a terrace which is shielded from the street by a masonry solar screen wall.

Living area—1,158 sq. ft., Lower level—608 sq. ft.

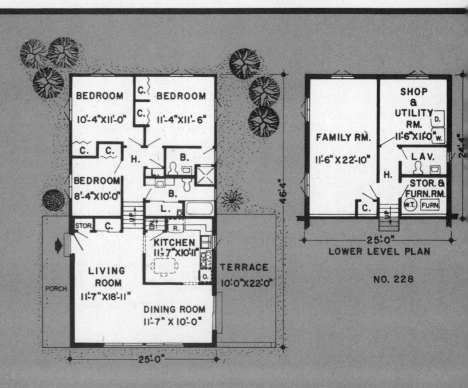

Hipped roof shelters economical plan

No. 132—Gently sloping forward to shade the front entrance, the hipped roof adds a cozy appeal to this two bedroom design. Comprising only 1075 square feet of living space, the home is economical to build, yet large and livable rooms and a bath and a bath and one half prove desirable extras. The kitchen is functional, opening to a small dining room and accessible to the garage and basement. The living room is spacious enough to set the scene for entertaining, and a large amount of wall space facilitates furniture arranging.

First floor—1,075 sq. ft., Basement—1,075 sq. ft.
Garage—460 sq. ft.

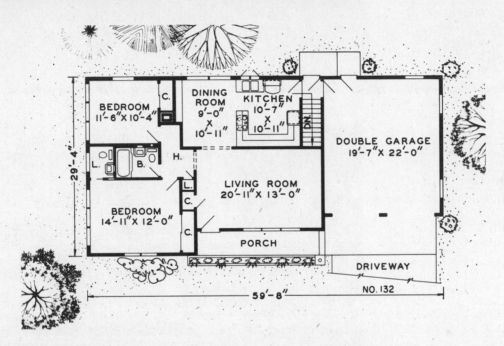

Family room opens to patio

No. 9530—This three bedroom ranch design has an excellent traffic pattern. Access to any room in the house is provided from the central hall. The family room and kitchen, feature open planning which tends to make the rooms appear even larger than they really are. An attractive breakfast bar serves as a divider. Sliding glass doors lead from the family room to the terrace. The basement stairs which have been placed in the garage lead to a full basement.

First floor—1,284 sq. ft., Basement—1,284 sq. ft. Garage—340 sq. ft.

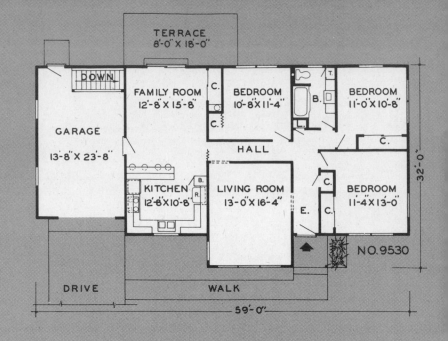

For large-scale entertaining

No. 9764—A very desirable floor plan design is found in this beautiful hipped roof home. The living room is especially nice with an attractive bow window and a corner type wood burning fireplace. The entrance foyer has a colorful slate floor. The master bedroom has a large walk-in closet as well as its own private bath with shower. The washer and dryer are located near the bedrooms for maximum efficiency. The open planned kitchen-family room area provides desirable space for many family activities.

First floor—1,534 sq. ft., Basement—1,534 sq. ft. Garage—447 sq. ft.

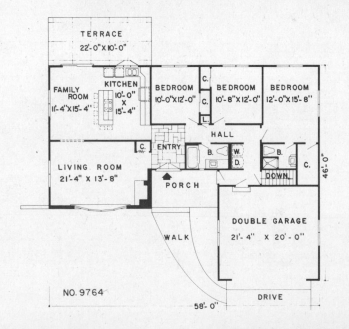

*For price and order information
see pages 108-109*

38

Ranch has exceptional plan

No. 9092—All rooms except the kitchen are accessible from the center hall. Plenty of light and ventilation are provided in all rooms. The living room and family room both have massive areas of glass. There are both inside and outside stairways to the basement. The kitchen is nicely arranged with space for eating and also for the washer and dryer. The rectangular shape of the house assures economy of construction.

First floor—1,670 sq. ft., Basement—1,670 sq. ft. Garage—570 sq. ft.

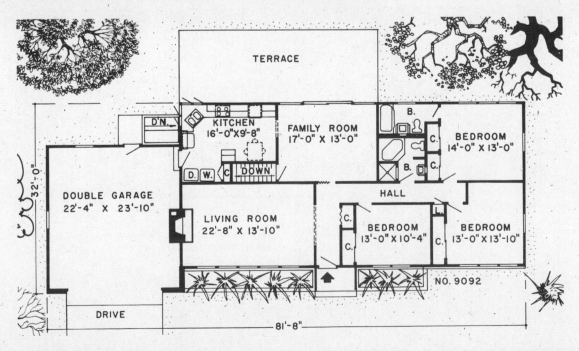

TERRACE

D'N. | KITCHEN 16'-0"X9'-8" | FAMILY ROOM 17'-0" X 13'-0" | B. | BEDROOM 14'-0" X 13'-0"

D. W. | C | DOWN

DOUBLE GARAGE 22'-4" X 23'-10"

32'-0"

LIVING ROOM 22'-8" X 13'-10"

HALL

BEDROOM 13'-0" X 10'-4"

BEDROOM 13'-0" X 13'-10"

NO. 9092

DRIVE

81'-8"

Kitchen-dining area saves space

No. 284—Merging the kitchen and dining area in this compact three bedroom plan is one of the features that makes this design work. Trimmed with red cedar shingles, the home boasts 1204 livable square feet and room for a growing family. A highly efficient bath is segmented by folding door and merits double sinks and built-in vanity. Living room is sizable and attaches a closet, and a utility room behind the garage offers laundry space.

First floor—1,204 sq. ft., Basement—1,168 sq. ft. Garage—234 sq. ft.

For price and order information see pages 108-109

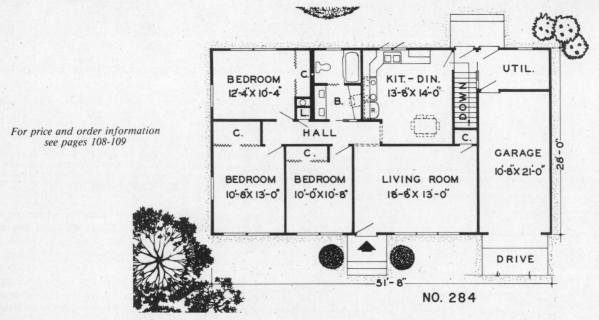

BEDROOM 12'-4" X 10'-4"
C.
KIT. - DIN. 13'-8" X 14'-0"
UTIL.
DOWN
B.
L.
C.
HALL
GARAGE 10'-8" X 21'-0"
28'-0"
BEDROOM 10'-8" X 13'-0"
BEDROOM 10'-0" X 10'-8"
C.
LIVING ROOM 18'-8" X 13'-0"
C.
DRIVE
51'-8"
NO. 284

Natural stone, brick adorn exterior

No. 266—Creative design combines stained plywood siding, Norman brick, and natural stone to fashion an exceptional exterior. Inside, the floor plan is neat and rooms large. Entrance hallway channels traffic, allowing the generous living room maximum privacy and the family room immediate access. Sleeping wing fills the right half of the home with three bedrooms, two full baths back-to-back, and a niche for laundry equipment. Family room and kitchen are separated by a convenient breakfast bar.

First floor—1,686 sq. ft., Basement—1,686 sq. ft. Garage—455 sq. ft.

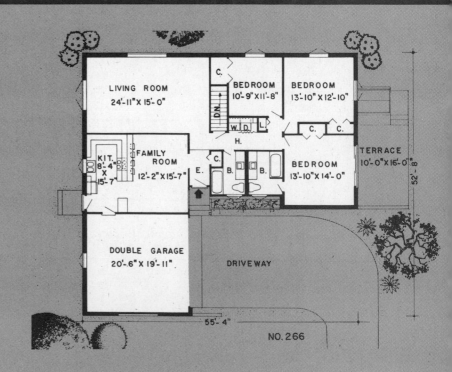

LIVING ROOM 24'-11" X 15'-0"
C.
BEDROOM 10'-9" X 11'-8"
BEDROOM 13'-10" X 12'-10"
DN.
W.
L.
C. C.
KIT. 8'-4" X 15'-7"
FAMILY ROOM 12'-2" X 15'-7"
H.
E.
B.
B.
BEDROOM 13'-10" X 14'-0"
TERRACE 10'-0" X 16'-0"
52'-8"
DOUBLE GARAGE 20'-6" X 19'-11".
DRIVEWAY
55'-4"
NO. 266

Budget rancher

No. 226—This California ranch design manages to include many advanced ideas but does it in a realistic manner, scaling them to a family budget. For example, note the sheltered entrance and entry. The entry blends into the central hall providing access to all rooms with a minimum of cross traffic. The kitchen is extra nice, containing washer and dryer space and many built-in cabinets and appliances. A snack bar separates the kitchen and dining room. The master bedroom is extra large and contains its own bathroom with shower.

First floor—1,372 sq. ft., Garage—460 sq. ft.

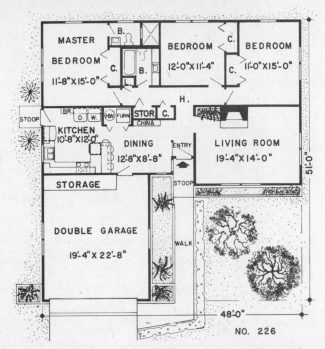

MASTER BEDROOM 11'-8"X15'-0"

BEDROOM 12'-0"X11'-4"

BEDROOM 11'-0"X15'-0"

KITCHEN 10'-8"X12'-0"

DINING 12'-8"X8'-8"

LIVING ROOM 19'-4"X14'-0"

STORAGE

DOUBLE GARAGE 19'-4" X 22'-8"

ENTRY

51'-0"

48'-0"

NO. 226

Many conveniences on a modern scale

No. 166—This small, compact split-level design has many of the conveniences usually found only in larger houses. Two full baths are located on the bedroom level, the one with shower is private to the master bedroom. The lower level family room is extra large and will provide an uncrowded area for many family activities. The large utility-storage room will be appreciated by the busy housewife.

Living area—1,088 sq. ft.
Family room — 543 sq. ft.

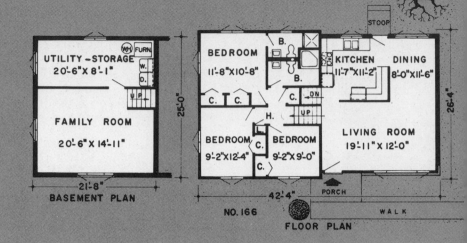

Low priced, loaded with features

No. 232—Brick veneer is used throughout on this low ranch design. This feature, combined with aluminum casement windows, will certainly keep maintenance at a minimum. Open planning is used in the kitchen-family room area. Notice how the kitchen is centrally located. The utility room contains the washer and dryer and additional space for storage. All bedroom closets are extra large and the master bedroom has a private bath.

First floor—1,421 sq. ft., Garage—488 sq. ft.

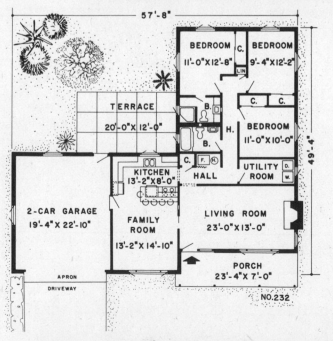

For price and order information
see pages 108-109

Efficient design conserves space

No. 372—Brick veneer trim and front gable greatly enhance the appearance of this modest home. Building economies are achieved through the use of a rectangular shape and a simple gable roof. Inside a large living room makes possible numerous furniture arrangements. A snack bar divides the kitchen and family room and sliding glass doors in the family room open onto a flagstone terrace. Utilities, storage and a recreation room can be added in the basement.

First floor—1,081 sq. ft., Basement—1,081 sq. ft. Garage—338 sq. ft.

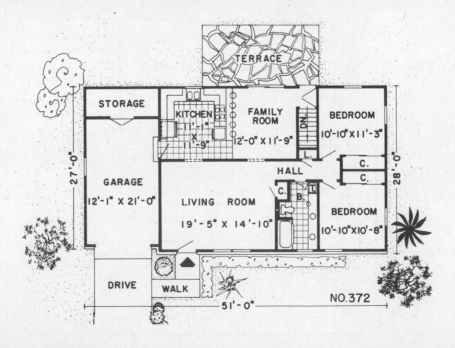

Cathedral ceilings add spaciousness

No. 9790—This house is both compact and livable and easy on the budget. Exterior maintenance is simplified by the low pitch of the roof and Redwood siding. The cut stone and cupola are items that add slightly to the cost but add greatly to the exterior beauty. The garage is extra long, providing a generous storage area at the rear. A full basement houses the utilities and provides space for a recreation room, etc.

First floor—1,131 sq. ft., Basement—1,131 sq. ft. Breezeway—312 sq. ft., Garage—392 sq. ft.

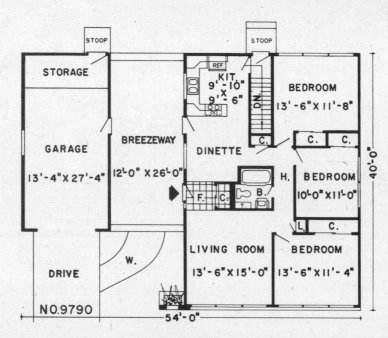

STOOP

STOOP

STORAGE

REF.

KIT
9'-10"
X
9'-6"

DN.

BEDROOM
13'-6"X11'-8"

GARAGE
13'-4"X 27'-4"

BREEZEWAY
12'-0" X 26'-0"

DINETTE

C.

C.

C.

H.

BEDROOM
10'-0"X11'-0"

F.

C.

B.

DRIVE

W.

LIVING ROOM
13'-6"X15'-0"

L.

C.

BEDROOM
13'-6"X11'-4"

NO. 9790

54'-0"

40'-0"

For price and order information see pages 108-109

Folding doors valuable addition

No. 156—Allowing the kitchen and coat closet to be closed off from the living room, the folding doors are one of the thoughtful additions that make this split foyer plan desirable. Besides the formal living room and dining room, a spacious family room is planned for family activities, and the well-closeted den might serve as a study, television room, or extra bedroom. Additional assets are the master bedroom with private bath, the extra large double garage, and the efficient kitchen with built-in broom closet.

Upper level—1,156 sq. ft., Lower level—583 sq. ft. Garage—528 sq. ft.

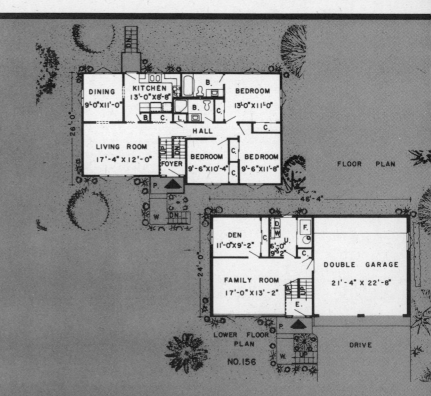

DINING
9'-0"X11'-0"

KITCHEN
13'-0"X8'-8"

B.

BEDROOM
13'-0"X11'-0"

B.

C.

HALL

B.

C.

L.

LIVING ROOM
17'-4"X12'-0"

FOYER

BEDROOM
9'-6"X10'-4"

BEDROOM
9'-6"X11'-8"

C.

FLOOR PLAN

46'-4"

26'-0"

DN

W

DEN
11'-0"X9'-2"

D.
W.

F.

U.

FAMILY ROOM
17'-0"X13'-2"

DOUBLE GARAGE
21'-4" X 22'-8"

E.

LOWER FLOOR PLAN

DRIVE

24'-0"

NO. 156

44

Double garage, workshop shown in plan

No. 9062—Covering only 1343 square feet of living space, this appealing brick-layered home, dominated by imposing brick chimney, offers a surprising amount of detail and includes full-sized double garage and adjacent workshop. Perhaps its most striking feature is the airy living room, bathed in light from windows flanking the wood-burning fireplace. Kitchen allots plentiful counter space and has access to separate dining room on one side and half bath on the other. Three bedrooms are nestled to the right of the entry and share a well-placed full bath.

**First floor—1,343 sq. ft., Basement—1,282 sq. ft.
Garage and storage—524 sq. ft.**

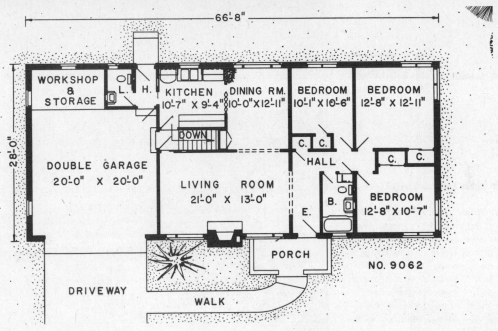

Garage doubles as family play area

No. 280—Here is a house that has been planned for an active, growing family on a budget. The floor plan reflects good planning with no waste space. Three bedrooms with large closets and two full baths are provided. The garage is designed to serve a dual purpose. The sliding glass doors at the rear admit lots of light, making the garage an excellent place for various activities. The living room at the rear of the house provides maximum privacy and a direct access to the patio through glass doors. A full basement is specified.

First floor—1,265 sq. ft., Basement—1,265 sq. ft. Garage—450 sq. ft.

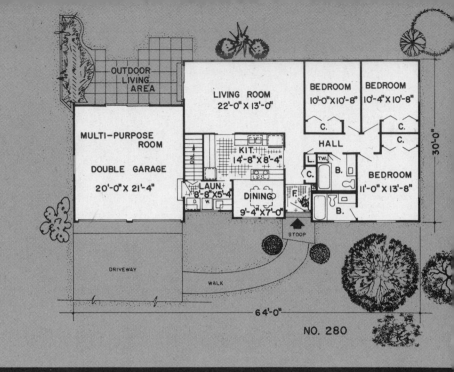

NO. 280

Hipped roof, fireplace lend appeal

No. 180—Exuding comfort and cozy warmth, this small stone design is enhanced by a hipped roof outside and fireplace within. A small family or retired couple will appreciate the interior arrangement. A utility room adjoining the kitchen provides space for laundry facilities close to the area where they are needed. Two bedrooms share the full hall bath, and the substantial kitchen apportions a dining area. The living room, complete with picture windows, affords a cheerful spot for relaxing around the fireside.

First floor—1,014 sq. ft.

For price and order information see pages 108-109

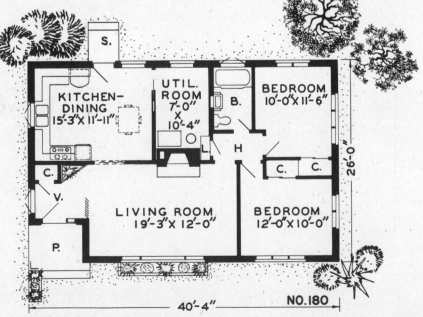

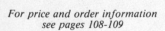

NO. 180

Basic design cuts construction costs

No. 212—Well-proportioned and rectangular shaped, this appealing ranch home boasts 1300 livable square feet and construction costs are kept to a minimum. The separate dining room radiates off the living room as well as a roomy kitchen with an option of including laundry euipment or a breakfast nook. Expenses are also reduced by the inclusion of the garage in the basement with enough remaining space for a utility room or workshop. Shake shingle siding and an abundance of windows create an attractive exterior image.

First floor—1,300 sq. ft., Basement—1,300 sq. ft.

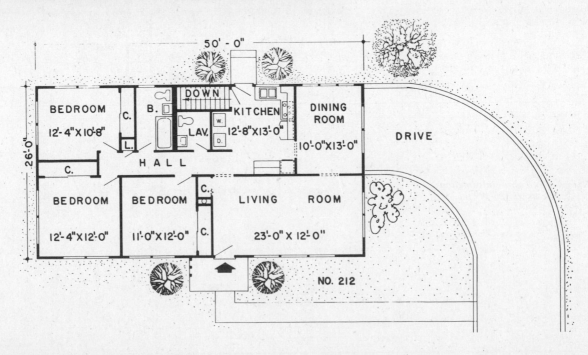

Brick retains style, value

No. 176—The entry to this lovely brick home is directly into the living room, which is graced with a wood-burning fireplace. Traffic from this room then is directed down a hall into the sleeping area or into the dining room. Adjacent to the dining room is a kitchen lined with cabinets and large enough to accommodate dining. The three bedroom plan is designed so that one bedroom could easily be converted to den or library. Adding space and protection to the gracious home is the complete basement.

First floor—1,470 sq. ft., Basement—1,470 sq. ft. Garage—342 sq. ft.

*For price and order information
see pages 108-109*

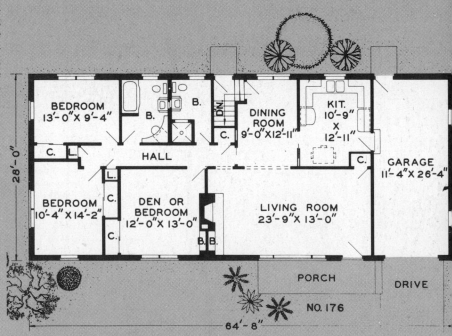

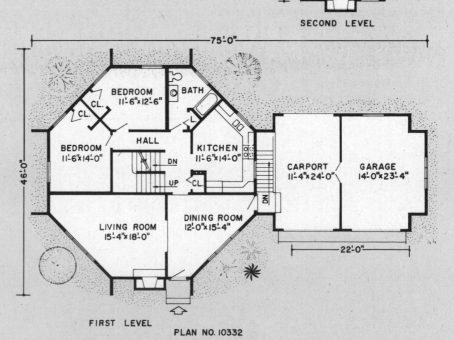

Master bedroom, den, fill second level

No. 10332—A spacious master bedroom with double closets and adjoining baths is steps from the cozy den with wood-burning fireplace on the upper level of this unique contemporary. Below, two additional bedrooms and living areas are grouped around a central hallway that allows access to the kitchen, bath, or living and dining rooms. Garage and carport are featured.

First floor—1,056 sq. ft.,
Second floor—736 sq. ft.
Basement—1,056 sq. ft.,
Garage—668 sq. ft.

*For price and order information
see pages 108-109*

SECOND LEVEL

CL.
M. BEDROOM
12'-4"x15'-4"
CL.
BATH
DN
CL.
DEN
15'-0"x15'-4"
40'-0"

FIRST LEVEL — **PLAN NO. 10332**

75'-0"
46'-0"
BEDROOM
11'-6"x12'-6"
BATH
CL.
CL.
BEDROOM
11'-6"x14'-0"
HALL
KITCHEN
11'-6"x14'-0"
DN
UP
CL.
CARPORT
11'-4"x24'-0"
GARAGE
14'-0"x23'-4"
LIVING ROOM
15'-4"x18'-0"
DINING ROOM
12'-0"x15'-4"
DN
22'-0"

Rustic ranch integrates outdoors

No. 10142—Appendaging a 31-foot redwood deck at rear and a long front porch, this ranch plan offers a woodsy appeal and plenty of involvement with the
outdoors. Inside, the floor plan caters to
the relaxed lifestyle of the seventies.
Flanking the large foyer is the spacious
sunken living room, warmed by a wood-
burning fireplace.

First floor—1,705 sq. ft.,
Basement—1,705 sq. ft.
Garage—576 sq. ft.

*For price and order information
see pages 108-109*

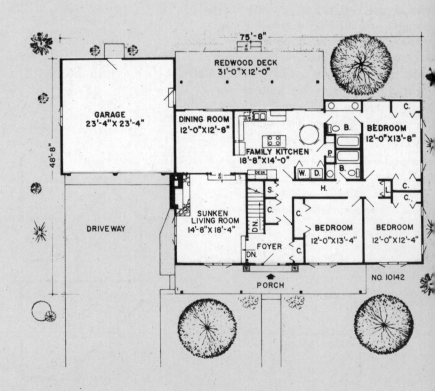

Balcony enriches facade, bedrooms

No. 10128—Two bedrooms enjoy a bonus in the 23-foot balcony that fronts this split level plan. Stone veneer, ornamental iron railings, and French doors create an eye-catching exterior, while effective zoning distinguishes the interior. Living areas are cozy and include firelit living room, well-proportioned dining room open to the terrace.

Living levels—1,344 sq. ft.
Garage levels—720 sq. ft.

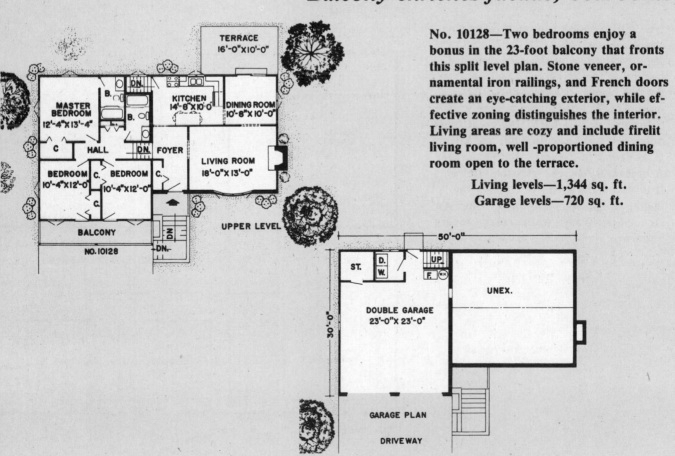

TERRACE 16'-0"x10'-0"

MASTER BEDROOM 12'-4"x13'-4"

KITCHEN 14'-8"x10'-0"

DINING ROOM 10'-8"x10'-0"

HALL FOYER

BEDROOM 10'-4"x12'-0"

BEDROOM 10'-4"x12'-0"

LIVING ROOM 18'-0"x13'-0"

BALCONY

NO. 10128

UPPER LEVEL

50'-0"

ST.

D. W.

UP

F.

DOUBLE GARAGE 23'-0"x 23'-0"

UNEX.

30'-0"

GARAGE PLAN

DRIVEWAY

51

Excellent first home

No. 28015—Solar storage cells on the south side contribute to the energy saving effectiveness of this well designed beginning family home. 3 bedrooms and 2 baths occupy the east wing. The master bedroom features a large walk-in closet and private bath. The great room opens out onto a patio while the kitchen gives access to the large double garage. A breakfast bar separates the kitchen from the living area while giving the feeling of spacious and open living. An air-lock entry adds to the energy saving features.

First floor—1,296 sq. ft.
Garage—484 sq. ft.

For price and order information
see pages 108-109

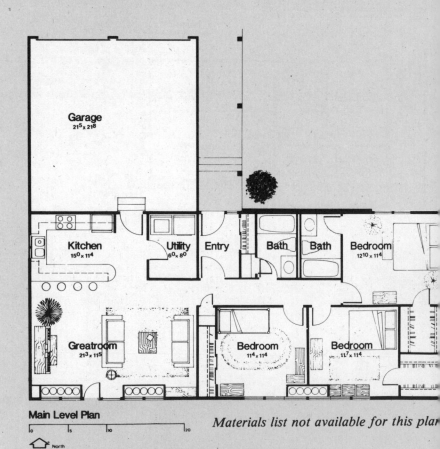

Main Level Plan

North

Materials list not available for this plan

garage
21³ x 21⁹

entry

NO. 28003

laundry

dining room
10⁴ x 11⁹

kitchen
10³ x 9⁰

bedroom
9⁹ x 10³

bedroom
12⁴ x 10³

clerestory above

great room
26⁹ x 11⁴

master bedroom
13⁶ x 12⁴

Floor Plan

0   5   10   20

⬆ North

wood frame
conc block
ceramic tile

Stucco masterpiece

No. 28003—A modified ranch design featuring a Great Room with a brick-accented wood burning stove. This stucco home has 3 bedrooms, 2 baths and a formal dining room all designed for a flat site with a north driveway. Among the energy conserving features are 2x6 exterior walls with R-19 insulation, an air-lock entry, and earth berming Passive solar gain through south windows and a large bank of clerestory windows.

**First floor—1,580 sq. ft.
Garage—515 sq. ft.**

Materials list not available for this plan.

Multi-level contemporary

No. 26111—The features of this multi-level contemporary home lend character to both the exterior and interior. A wooden deck skirts most of three sides. Great variety in the size and shape of doors and windows is apparent. Inside the living room forms a unique living center. It can be reached from sliding glass doors from the deck or down several steps from the main living level inside. It is overlooked by a low balcony from the entryway and dining room on the lower level and from the second floor landing. Large windows on both the right and left keep it well lit. A fireplace here is optional Ceilings slope upward two stories. A partial basement is located below the design.

First floor—769 sq. ft.
Second floor—572 sq. ft.

*For price and order information
see pages 108-109*

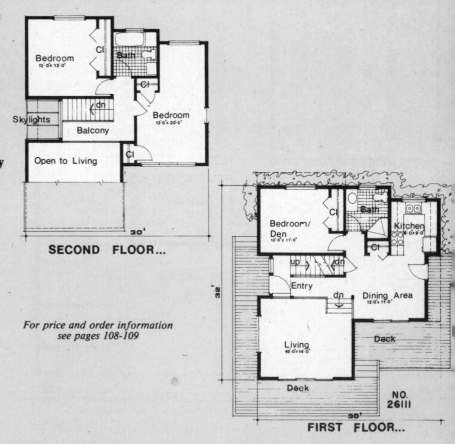

SECOND FLOOR...

FIRST FLOOR...

54

Passive contemporary design features sunken living room

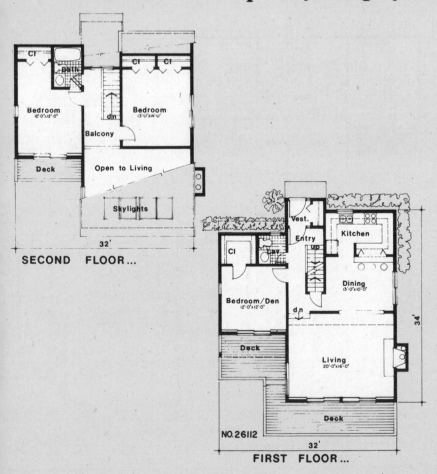

SECOND FLOOR...

CI

BATH

Bedroom
12'-0"x12'-0"

CI CI

Bedroom
13'-0"x14'-0"

Balcony

dn

Deck

Open to Living

Skylights

32'

FIRST FLOOR...

Vest.

Entry
up

Kitchen

CI

Lav.

Bedroom/Den
12'-0"x12'-0"

dn

Dining
13'-0"x10'-0"

Deck

Living
20'-0"x16'-0"

Deck

NO. 26112

32'

34'

No. 26112—Wood adds its warmth to the contemporary features of this passive design. Generous use of southern glass doors and windows, an air lock entry, skylights and a living room fireplace reduce energy needs. R-26 insulation is shown for floors and sloping ceilings. Decking rims the front of the home and gives access through sliding glass doors to a bedroom/den area and living room. The dining room lies up several steps from the living room and is separated from it by a half wall. The dining room flows into the kitchen through an eating bar. A second floor landing balcony overlooks the living room. Two bedrooms, one with its own private deck, and a full bath finish the second level.

First floor—911 sq. ft.
Second floor—560 sq. ft.

55

Passive solar and contemporary features

No. 26110—Numerous southern glass doors and windows, skylights and a greenhouse clue the exterior viewer of the passive solarness of this contemporary design. For minimum heat loss, 2x6 studs for R-19 insulation are shown in exterior walls and R-33 insulation is shown in all sloping ceilings. The living room employs a concrete slab floor for solar gain. Basement space is located under the kitchen, dining room, lower bedroom and den. A northern entrance through a verstibule and French doors channels you upward to the first floor living area. A unique feature on this level is the skylit living room ceiling which slants two stories. Second story rooms are lit by clerestory windows. Two balconies are on this level, and exterior one off the bedroom and an interior one overlooking the living room.

First floor—902 sq. ft.
Second floor-567 sq. ft.

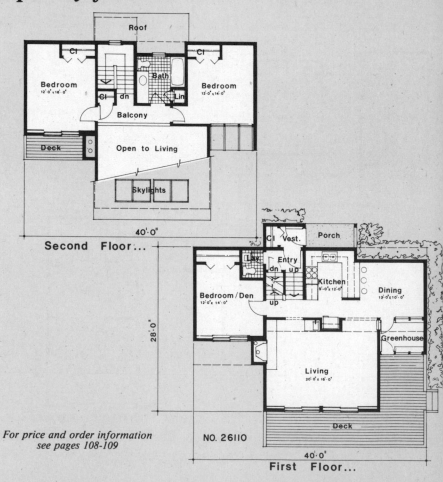

*For price and order information
see pages 108-109*

56

Triple dormers distinguish plan

No. 10354—Dormers extend the upstairs bedrooms and bath and add interest to the facade of this two level design. Traditional charm pervades the interior as well, with the kitchen opening to a 21-ft. screened porch, ideal for dining or napping. The first floor master bedroom shows double closets and adjoins a full bath, and the family room merits a wood-burning fireplace and sliding glass doors to the deck. Also included are the formal living room at left of the foyer and the upstairs playroom with extra large storage closets.

First floor—1,188 sq. ft.,
Second floor—834 sq. ft.
Basement—1,140 sq. ft.,
Garage—498 sq. ft.

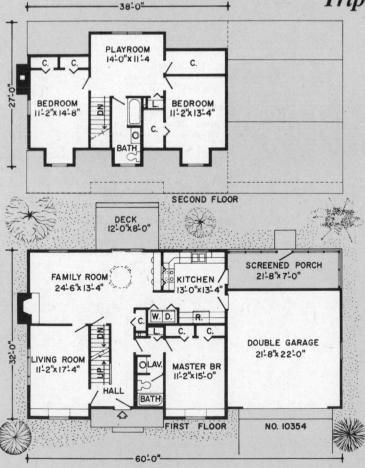

57

Fireplace center of circular living area

No. 10274—A dramatically positioned fireplace forms the focus of the main living area in this single level contemporary. Kitchen, dining, and living rooms form a circle that allows work areas to flow into living areas and outdoors, via sliding glass doors, to the wood deck. Three large bedrooms and two full baths are grouped in a wing away from the living areas. Tucked off the kitchen is a laundry room with closet.

Living area—1,783 sq. ft.,
Garage—576 sq. ft.

*For price and order information
see pages 108-109*

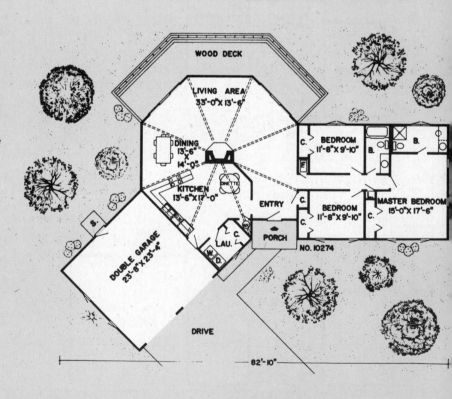

Fight the high cost of energy

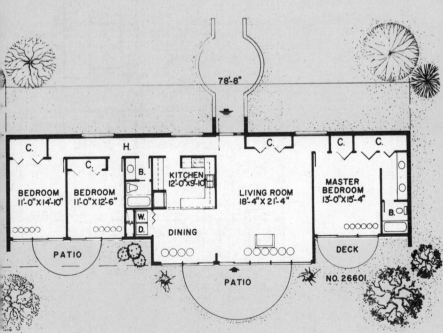

No. 26601—This striking contemporary passive solar home, designed for a growing family, can help combat run-away fuel bills. Large expanses of glass on the south side warms the house during the day while storing heat in solar water tubes positioned behind windows for heat at night. Master bedroom has private bath and a redwood deck. Living room, dining room and kitchen are the central attractions in this well zoned home. Sliding glass doors give access to the patio from both the living room and dining room. Two bedrooms share a patio accessible from each room via sliding glass doors. The north side of the house is bermed up with earth for protection from cold north winds. Super insulation in walls and ceiling complete this energy efficient, economical home.

Living area—1,748 sq. ft.

Apartment suite featured

No. 10374—Passive solar details highlight this home. From the solar greenhouse and many southern windows and doors to concrete slab construction, few northern windows and air-lock entry, it emphasizes energy efficiency. Concrete floor and walls and water filled barrels gather heat in the greenhouse area. The first floor plan includes a kitchen/dining area, living room with wood burning stove, two bedrooms and one and half baths. The larger of the two bedrooms has a large walk-in closet and a windowed seat area. A mother-in-law suite or apartment, complete with kitchen, full bath, walk-in closet with dressing area, built-in dresser, living area and balcony fill the second floor. Detailed drawings are included for front deck and garden area.

First floor—1,284 sq. ftt
Second floor—254 sq. ft.
Basement—193 sq. ft.
Garage—664 sq. ft.

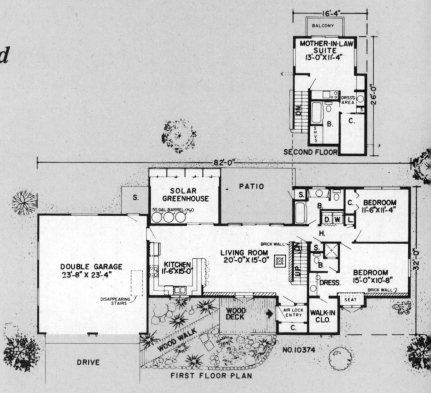

For price and order information
see pages 108-109

Energy efficient plan uses berms

No. 10358—Semi-underground to save energy, this handsome design calls for soil bermed up to the cornices on sides and back and an airlock type vestibule. Plenty of warm sunlight penetrates the well-windowed front, designed to face south, and rear and side window wells allow for emergency exits. For family-oriented livability, the great room with wood-burning fireplace merges with the dining area, and a functional corridor kitchen is handy to both. Located off the double garage, the mudroom functions as a laundry and utility area. Three large bedrooms share two full baths.

**First floor—1,620 sq. ft.,
Garage—448 sq. ft.**

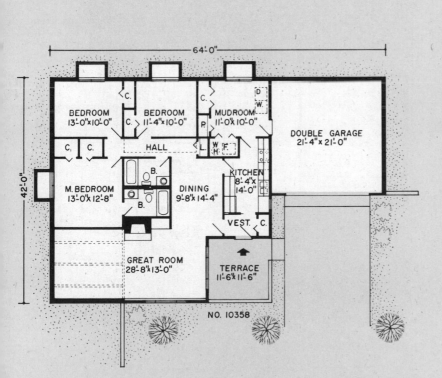

64'-0"

42'-0"

BEDROOM
13'-0"x10'-0"

BEDROOM
11'-4"x10'-0"

MUDROOM
11'-0"x10'-0"

DOUBLE GARAGE
21'-4" x 21'-0"

C.

HALL

M. BEDROOM
13'-0"x12'-8"

DINING
9'-8"x14'-4"

KITCHEN
8'-4"x
14'-0"

B.

B.

GREAT ROOM
28'-8"x13'-0"

VEST.

C.

TERRACE
11'-6"x11'-6"

NO. 10358

Tasteful elegance aim of design

No. 22020—With an exterior that expresses French Provincial charm, this single level design emphasizes elegance and offers a semi-circular dining area overlooking the patio. To pamper parents, the master bedroom annexes a long dressing area and private bath, while another bath serves the second and third bedrooms. A wood-burning fireplace furnishes the family room.

House proper—1,772 sq. ft.
Garage—469 sq. ft.

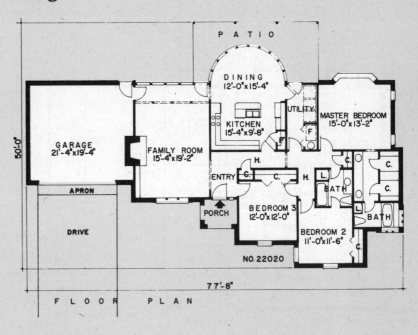

*For price and order information
see pages 108-109*

Plan boasts accommodating kitchen

No. 1008—Handy to patio, family room
and living room, the kitchen in this
home offers a snack bar and a garage
entrance. Convenience marks the entire
plan, which supplies a closeted entrance
foyer to channel traffic. Warm and
cozy, the family room is furnished with
wood-burning fireplace. Three ample
bedrooms share two full baths.

First floor—1,510 sq. ft.
Storage room—108 sq. ft.
Carport—417 sq. ft.

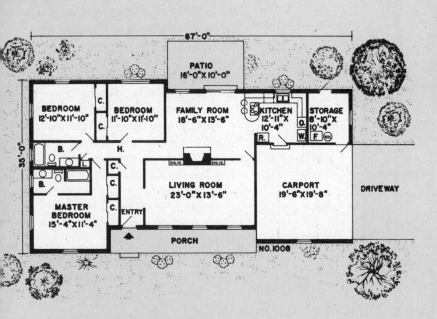

Small but versatile passive design

No. 26092—This house is well suited as a vacation home or for a small family. The One Design Waterwall passive solar system is employed in the southern walls. R-23 insulation is used in exterior walls, R-19 in the floors and R-30 in the ceilings. An air lock entry and coniferous trees on the north side for a winter windbreak further add to energy efficiency. Clerestory windows allow the sun's warmth to enter. The entryway with adjoining storage space directs you into the fireplaced living room or out onto the deck. A kitchen and dining room are also on this level. Two bedrooms and a full bath lie up several steps.

Living area—925 sq. ft.
Entry & Storage—80 sq. ft.

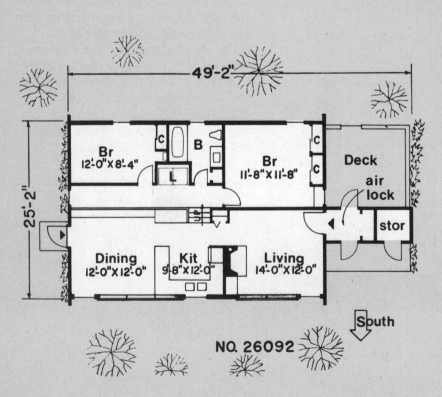

NO. 26092

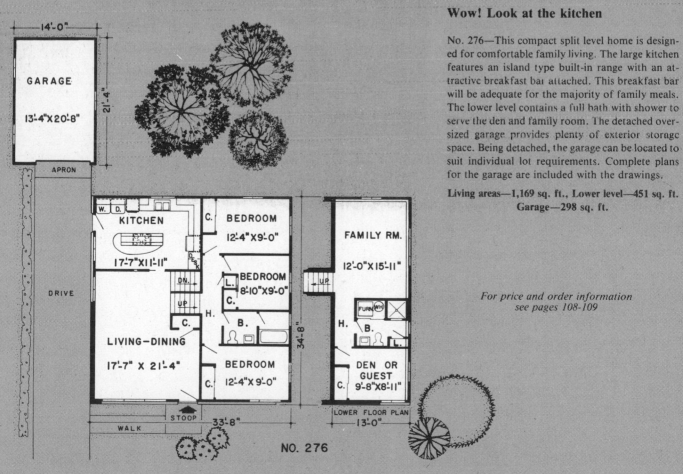

Wow! Look at the kitchen

No. 276—This compact split level home is design-ed for comfortable family living. The large kitchen features an island type built-in range with an attractive breakfast bar attached. This breakfast bar will be adequate for the majority of family meals. The lower level contains a full bath with shower to serve the den and family room. The detached over-sized garage provides plenty of exterior storage space. Being detached, the garage can be located to suit individual lot requirements. Complete plans for the garage are included with the drawings.

Living areas—1,169 sq. ft., Lower level—451 sq. ft. Garage—298 sq. ft.

For price and order information
see pages 108-109

GARAGE
13'-4" X 20'-8"

14'-0"
21'-4"

APRON

DRIVE

W. D.
KITCHEN
17'-7" X 11'-11"
C.
BEDROOM
12'-4" X 9'-0"

DN.
UP

BEDROOM
8'-10" X 9'-0"
L.
C.

H.

C.

LIVING—DINING
17'-7" X 21'-4"

B.

BEDROOM
12'-4" X 9'-0"
C.

WALK
STOOP
33'-8"

34'-8"

UP

FAMILY RM.
12'-0" X 15'-11"

FURN WH

H.
B.
L.

DEN OR
GUEST
9'-8" X 8'-11"
C.

LOWER FLOOR PLAN
13'-0"

NO. 276

65

Hall bath convenient for guests

No. 9746—Accessible to the large living room, the half bath is a decided asset in this floor plan since it provides both a powder room for guests and an extra family bath. Dining room and living room will share the restful mood created by the wood-burning fireplace, and the kitchen, open on both ends, skirts the dining area. The carport entryway also opens on the side terrace which fringes two of the bedrooms.

First floor—1,167 sq. ft., Basement—1,121 sq. ft.
Carport and storage—495 sq. ft.

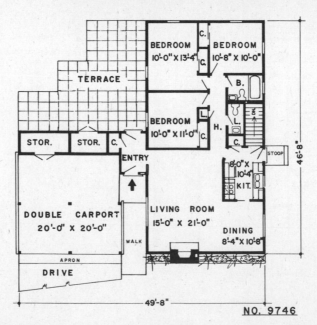

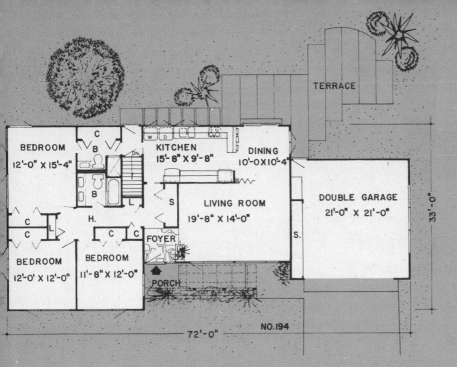

BEDROOM
12'-0" X 15'-4"

KITCHEN
15'-8" X 9'-8"

DINING
10'-0" X 10'-4"

DOUBLE GARAGE
21'-0" X 21'-0"

LIVING ROOM
19'-8" X 14'-0"

BEDROOM
12'-0" X 12'-0"

BEDROOM
11'-8" X 12'-0"

FOYER

PORCH

TERRACE

33'-0"

72'-0"

NO. 194

House made for young families

No. 194—This living room and dining room flow together, giving an effect of great spaciousness, however, the two rooms can be divided when desirable with the folding partition. There are three bedrooms of adequate size and two complete bath rooms. Laundry space is shown in the kitchen for conveneience. A double garage provides shelter for the car and also contains a large storage closet.

**First floor—1,461 sq. ft., Basement—815 sq. ft.
Garage—462 sq. ft.**

Perfect for small lot

No. 9508—This house was designed so that the breezeway and garage can be omitted without detracting from the appearance of the house. By omitting them the house can be built on a very narrow lot. The housewife can certainly see what is going on from the kitchen. The four casement windows will provide more than adequate light and ventilation. Two full bathrooms are provided. The one with shower is very convenient to the master bedroom, kitchen and rear service door.

**First floor—1,269 sq. ft., Basement—1,269 sq. ft.
Garage—336 sq. ft.**

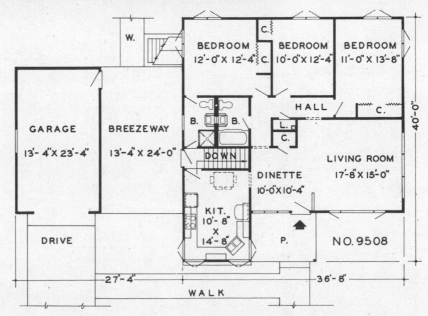

*For price and order information
see pages 108-109*

GARAGE
13'-4" X 23'-4"

BREEZEWAY
13'-4" X 24'-0"

BEDROOM
12'-0" X 12'-4"

BEDROOM
10'-0" X 12'-4"

BEDROOM
11'-0" X 13'-8"

HALL

DOWN

DINETTE
10'-0" X 10'-4"

LIVING ROOM
17'-8" X 15'-0"

KIT.
10'-8" X 14'-8"

DRIVE

P.

NO. 9508

40'-0"

27'-4"

36'-8"

WALK

Planned for family comfort

No. 9592—Here's a wonderfully functional plan with much more living space than is usually found in a house which is only forty feet wide. The double entrance doors and mid-level foyer add an air of luxury to the exterior appearance. Two full baths are provided, one on each level. The wood panelled family room is very large and will undoubtedly be the most popular area in the house. The furnace and water heater are centrally located for maximum efficiency and economy of construction.

Living area—1,148 sq. ft., Family room—467 sq. ft. Garage—681 sq. ft.

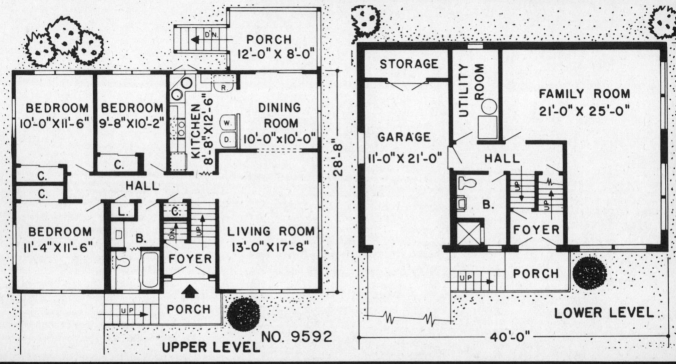

UPPER LEVEL   NO. 9592

LOWER LEVEL

Budget design shows three bedrooms

No. 340—Modest in square footage, this rectangular ranch style allows for economy of construction while providing plenty of room for a growing family. Three bedrooms occupy the right of the plan, with full bath centrally located for efficiency. Tucked within the elongated kitchen/dining area is a handy laundry niche, and storage space is shown behind the garage and in the full basement, a potential site for a family or recreation room. An appealing touch is added by the roofed front porch.

First floor—1,055 sq. ft., Basement—1,055 sq. ft. Garage—274 sq. ft.

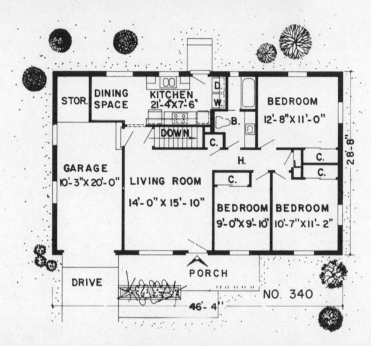

For price and order information see pages 108-109

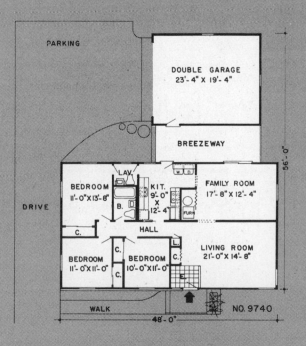

Designed for narrow lot

No. 9740—By placing the garage at the rear, this contemporary home can be built on a narrower than average lot. The parking area then can be used as patio or terrace. The width of the breezeway between the house and garage can be varied according to lot depth. The three bedroom plan includes a bath and one-half. The furnace and hot water heater are hidden behind an accordion door in the family room, which opens onto the breezeway. The tiled entryway provides direct access to the living room.

First floor—1,344 sq. ft., Garage—480 sq. ft.

69

Dining room annexes roofed terrace

No. 9722—Ideal for outdoor dining, the roofed terrace in this contemporary home is separated from the dining room by sliding glass doors. The dining room, kitchen, and family room are placed to take advantage of the terrace. Lined with built-in shelves and a corner fireplace, the living room provides a more formal setting for welcoming guests. The three bedrooms include a master bedroom provided with a spacious bath and shower that also opens to the family room. A full basement is outlined.

First floor—1,480 sq. ft., Basement—1,480 sq. ft. Garage—433 sq. ft.

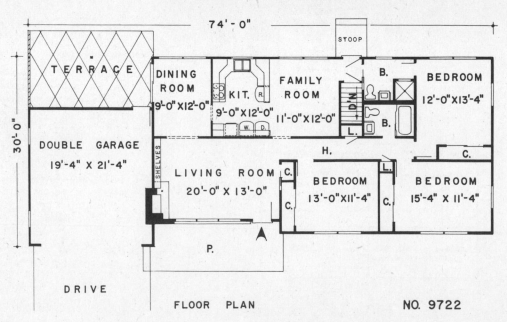

FLOOR PLAN   NO. 9722

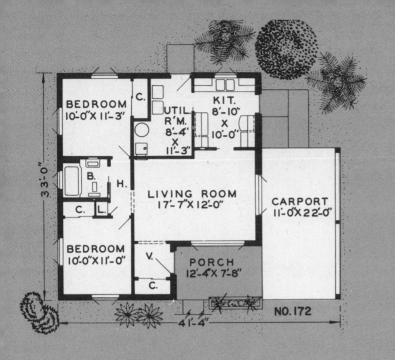

Western flat-top neat, businesslike

No. 172—Slung low to the ground, this Western design clothed in brick presents an orderly and interesting image. An excellent arrangement of rooms begins with the foyer off the shaded porch and includes two bedrooms separated by bath and linen closet, a well-ordered kitchen, and a central living room. A large utility room with washer and dryer space flanks the kitchen and would provide room for a canned goods pantry or a freezer.

First floor—885 sq. ft., Carport—242 sq. ft.

Shielded terrace moves living outdoors

No. 224—Roomy and completely private, a 26 foot terrace edges and opens to the living room and family room of this California ranch, drawing family activities outdoors. Textured with brick, heavy battens, and a shake shingle roof, the well-proportioned plan clusters kitchen, family-dining, and living rooms near the terrace. Bedrooms fill the left half of the home, and back-to-back baths serve the area. Storage space is generous, including inside closets and a storage room behind the terrace.

First floor—1,544 sq. ft., Terrace—324 sq. ft.

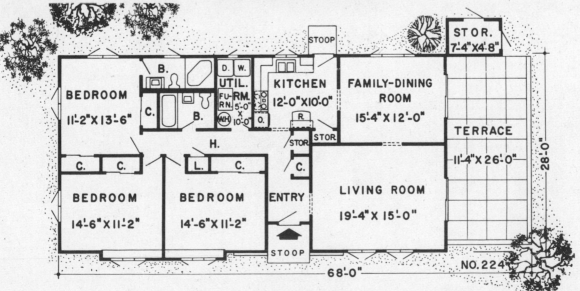

*For price and order information
see pages 108-109*

Hipped roof harmonizes with brick

No. 182—Presenting a warm, engaging exterior, this three bedroom home combines brick and a hipped roof and adds a generous sprinkling of windows. Fireplace and picture window pour light into the living room, which meets a formal dining room. Designed for both dining and cooking, the kitchen is large and accessible to basement, rear yard, and den or bedroom, which enjoys a half bath. Two more bedrooms, plus a compartmented bath with double sinks, are provided.

First floor—1,521 sq. ft., Basement—1,521 sq. ft.

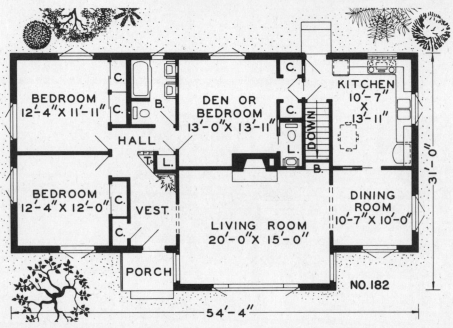

Mud room sample of plan's efficiency

No. 332—Expert planning maximizes livable space in this sleek L-shaped contemporary. Backing the elongated garage is a mud room that effectively combines laundry center, half bath, and utility area. Kitchen and family room beyond share, via sliding glass doors, a terrace perfect for sunning and picnicking.

First floor—1,324 sq. ft., Garage—298 sq. ft.

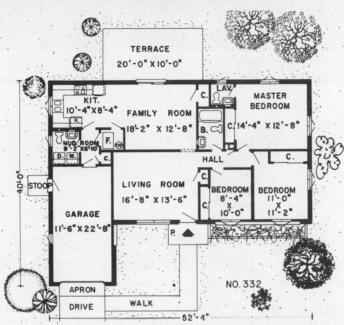

TERRACE
20'-0" X 10'-0"

KIT.
10'-4"X8'-4"

FAMILY ROOM
18'-2" X 12'-8"

LAV.

MASTER BEDROOM
14'-4" X 12'-8"

MUD ROOM
9'-2"X6'-10"

HALL

LIVING ROOM
16'-8" X 13'-6"

BEDROOM
8'-4" X 10'-0"

BEDROOM
11'-0" X 11'-2"

GARAGE
11'-6" X 22'-8"

STOOP

APRON

DRIVE

WALK

NO. 332

52'-4"

40'-0"

*For price and order information
see pages 108-109*

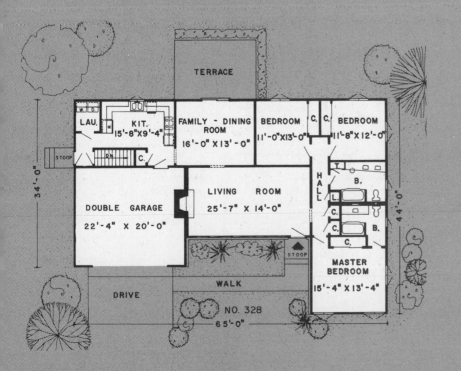

TERRACE

LAU.

KIT.
15'-8"X9'-4"

FAMILY - DINING ROOM
16'-0" X 13'-0"

BEDROOM
11'-0"X13'-0"

BEDROOM
11'-8" X 12'-0"

LIVING ROOM
25'-7" X 14'-0"

DOUBLE GARAGE
22'-4" X 20'-0"

HALL

B.

STOOP

MASTER BEDROOM
15'-4" X 13'-4"

DRIVE

WALK

NO. 328

34'-0"

44'-0"

65'-0"

Stone chimney punctuates exterior

No. 328—Cut stone sheathes the chimney and side of this dignified ranch style and imparts distinction and character to the exterior. Inside, entry is into the large living room, bathed in light from a glowing wood-burning fireplace. Family-dining room beyond opens to terrace via sliding glass doors, and adjoining kitchen complex etches a compact laundry room. Three bedrooms, two full baths, and copious closet space comprise the sleeping area, and master bedroom enjoys a private bath.

**First floor—1,757 sq. ft., Basement—1,757 sq. ft.
Garage—467 sq. ft.**

Stone, railing color exterior

No. 312—Cut stone and ornamental iron railing and columns lace the exterior of this porch-fronted plan and add interest to its basic rectangular shape. Segregated foyer with coat closet meets the sizable living room, and attached den supplies an ideal playroom or television room. Beyond the living room, an informal family room is bordered by U-shaped kitchen with access to garage and rear yard. Double garage is edged by a lockable storage room, perfect for bicycles and lawnmowers.

First floor—1,386 sq. ft., Garage—416 sq. ft.

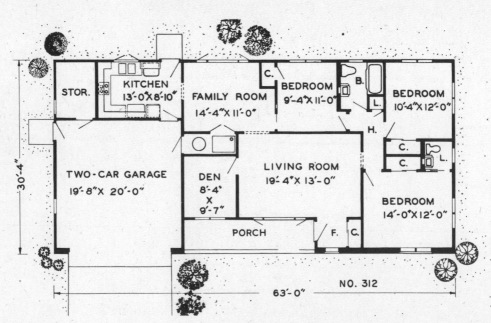

STOR.

KITCHEN
13'-0"X 8'-10"

FAMILY ROOM
14'-4"X 11'-0"

C.

BEDROOM
9'-4"X 11'-0"

B.

L.

BEDROOM
10'-4"X 12'-0"

TWO-CAR GARAGE
19'-8"X 20'-0"

DEN
8'-4"
X
9'-7"

LIVING ROOM
19'-4"X 13'-0"

H.

C.

C.

L.

BEDROOM
14'-0"X 12'-0"

30'-4"

PORCH

F.

C.

63'-0"

NO. 312

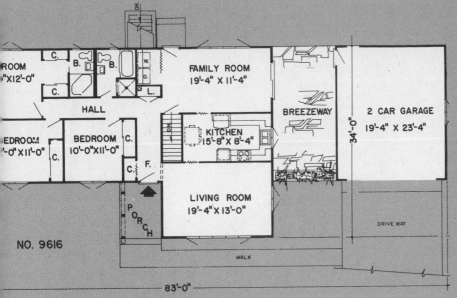

NO. 9616

Gracious living for less

No. 9616—This house is not nearly as large or costly as it appears to be. The house alone contains only 1,448 square feet. If you have a large lot but a limited budget this may be the house for you. Plenty of large size closets are provided as well as two full baths. The master bedroom bath contains an attractive square tub which will please the lady of the house. The "U" shaped kitchen is efficiently arranged and contains a generous size eating area.

**First floor—1,448 sq. ft., Basement—1,448 sq. ft.
Garage—480 sq. ft.**

Family room heart of ranch

No. 192—Being rectangular in shape, this house will be economical to build. Note how the master bedroom is separated from the other bedrooms for maximum privacy. It contains a complete bathroom and a seven foot closet. The kitchen is the nucleus of this design which makes it only a few steps to any room in the house including the garage and basement. Sliding glass doors completely cover the rear wall of the family room and lead out to a colorful flagstone terrace.

**First floor—1,350 sq. ft., Basement—1,350 sq. ft.
Garage—414 sq. ft.**

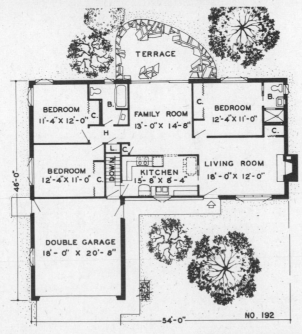

*For price and order information
see pages 108-109*

75

Simple, carefree living

No. 9506—This house was designed for a narrow lot. It has many attractive features. Three bedrooms and two full baths are provided. Although a full basement is specified, washer and dryer space is provided in the kitchen to save the housewife many steps. The family room is conveniently located near the kitchen and opens onto a flagstone terrace. The cut stone planter and flagstone approach at the front entrance are very attractive.

First floor—1,446 sq. ft., Basement—1,446 sq. ft. Garage—217 sq. ft.

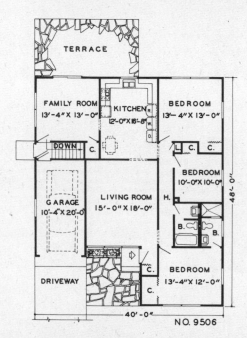

Living space camouflaged in neat plan

No. 376—Arranging bedrooms to the rear and garage doors to the side yields a clean, appealing facade in this contemporary plan and camouflages a surprising amount of space. From the inside the foyer, living and family rooms are equally accessible and help separate formal and informal activities. Larger of the two is the family room, bordering the compact kitchen, terrace, and stairway to the basement. Two full baths benefit the bedroom wing, which comprises three bedrooms and adequate closet space. Full basement and oversized garage provide plentiful storage space.

**First floor—1,387 sq. ft., Basement—1,355 sq. ft.
Garage—553 sq. ft.**

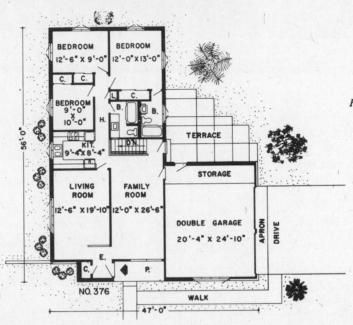

*For price and order information
see pages 108-109*

Two baths furnish moderate brick

No. 124—Two full baths, one private to the double-closeted master bedroom, indicate just one of the luxury assets in this modest brick trimmed ranch. Tiled foyer spills into the living room and allows an efficient traffic pattern. Open to dining area and divided only by breakfast bar, the compact kitchen adjoins a laundry center and is accessible to the terrace. Liberal storage area is provided in the double garage, and a full basement will fill additional needs.

**First floor—1,255 sq. ft., Basement—1,215 sq. ft.
Garage—462 sq. ft.**

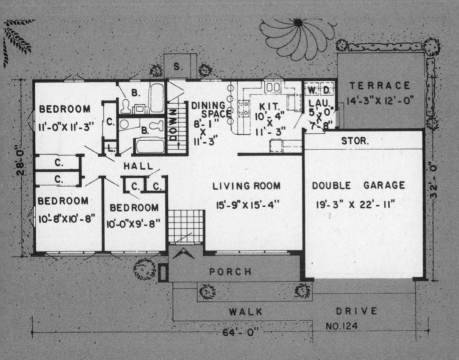

Contemporary plan styled for activity

No. 334—Generously proportioned rooms, cathedral ceilings, and a sunken family room create an airy, spacious design that sets the mood for family activity. Built around convenience, this brick-trimmed contemporary calls for an open kitchen/dining area with snack bar and an adjoining utility room for laundry chores. Three bedrooms and two full baths edge the plan, and the 20-foot living room is augmented by the large, vinyl-tiled family room, complete with sliding glass doors to the terrace.

**First floor—1,486 sq. ft., Family room—301 sq. ft.
Garage — 576 sq. ft.**

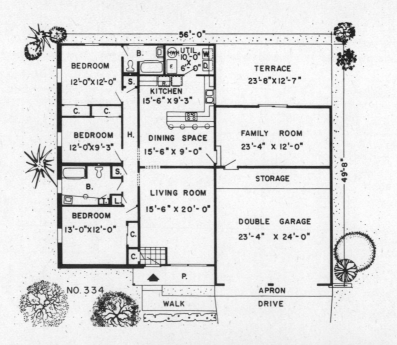

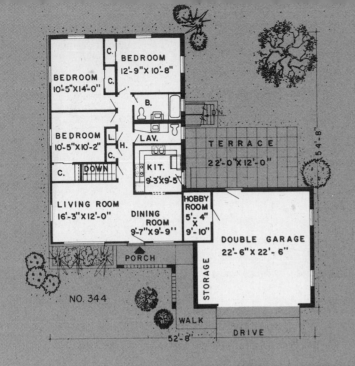

NO. 344

Floor plan labels:
- BEDROOM 10'-5"x14'-0"
- BEDROOM 12'-9"x10'-8"
- BEDROOM 10'-5"x10'-2"
- LAV.
- KIT. 9'-3"x9'-5"
- TERRACE 22'-0"x12'-0"
- LIVING ROOM 16'-3"x12'-0"
- DINING ROOM 9'-7"x9'-9"
- HOBBY ROOM 5'-4"x9'-10"
- DOUBLE GARAGE 22'-6"x22'-6"
- STORAGE
- PORCH
- DOWN
- WALK
- DRIVE
- 52'-8"
- 54'-8"

Compact plan enjoys hobby room

No. 344—Three bedrooms, one and one half baths, and even a hobby room are included in this compact plan, trimmed in face brick and vertical siding. By eliminating unnecessary hallways, this design embodies good planning and achieves maximum use of its 1147 square feet of living area. Bedrooms are served by a full bath, backed by a half bath placed to accommodate both living and sleeping areas. Separate dining room is supplemented by a terrace with access to the kitchen for ease in catering family barbecues.

First floor—1,147 sq. ft., Basement—1,147 sq. ft. Garage and hobby room—590 sq. ft.

Mid-sized ranch chooses roofed terrace

No. 346—Sporting generously-proportioned living areas, this moderate ranch style extends recreation and relaxation areas onto the covered terrace, open to the family room via sliding glass doors. More formal gatherings are slated for the sizable living room, with atmosphere contributed by glowing wood-burning fireplace. Traffic is expertly channeled through the foyer, allowing immediate access to the zoned bedroom wing. Three bedrooms fill the area, which allots copious storage space and a full bath for use of the master bedroom.

First floor—1,579 sq. ft., Basement—1,579 sq. ft. Garage—504 sq. ft.

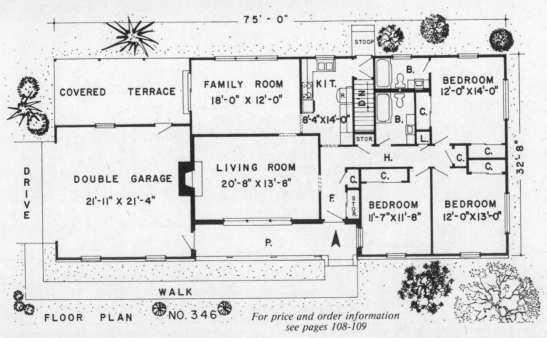

Floor plan labels:
- COVERED TERRACE
- FAMILY ROOM 18'-0" X 12'-0"
- KIT. 8'-4"X14'-0"
- BEDROOM 12'-0"X14'-0"
- DOUBLE GARAGE 21'-11" X 21'-4"
- LIVING ROOM 20'-8" X 13'-8"
- BEDROOM 11'-7"X11'-8"
- BEDROOM 12'-0"X13'-0"
- STOOP
- STOR
- DRIVE
- WALK
- 75'-0"
- 32'-8"

FLOOR PLAN — NO. 346 *For price and order information see pages 108-109*

House for today's people

No. 368—A striking modern exterior sets the tone carried forth by the large family room with a fireplace, the adjacent stone patio, the horseshoe shaped kitchen with 11½ feet of counter space, the large, centrally located bath with two sinks, and the three bedrooms. That tone, so prevalent, is today.

**First floor—1,612 sq. ft., Basement—1,308 sq. ft.
Garage—540 sq. ft.**

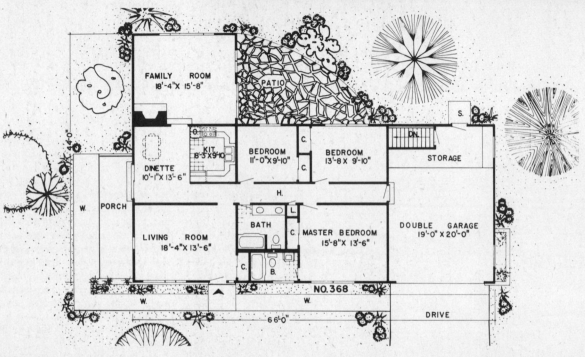

Additions transform traditional plan

No. 152—Intriguing diamond light windows, contrasting siding, and a cupola trim convert this simple ranch style into an appealing design. Its expansive living room enjoys both a fireplace and a terrace, via sliding glass doors. The kitchen is compact and handy to the formal dining room and garage. Three bedrooms comprise the sleeping wing, including a master bedroom with private bath, and a niche is provided for the washer and dryer. Boat storage is included in the extra large garage.

First floor—1,643 sq. ft., Basement—1,643 sq. ft. Garage—763 sq. ft.

For price and order information see pages 108-109

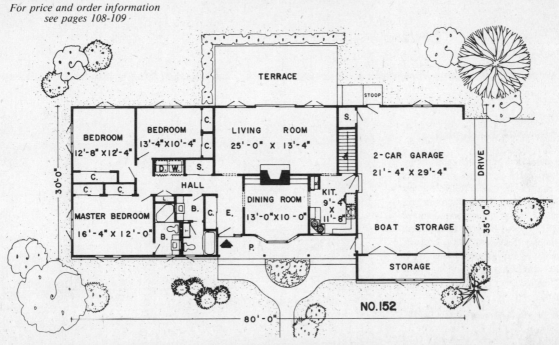

NO. 152

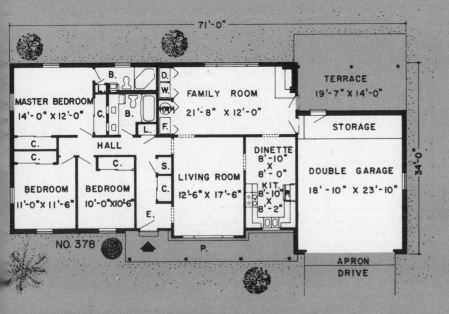

Ranch style emphasizes livability

No. 378—Two full baths, plentiful closet space, and an expansive, well-arranged family room show the emphasis is on living in this three bedroom plan. The basic ranch plan offers one-floor convenience, improved by the closeted foyer and hallway which yield an efficient traffic pattern. Reserved for formality, the living room borders kitchen and dining areas and is supplemented by a family room that extends over 21 feet.

First floor—1,560 sq. ft., Garage—501 sq. ft.

Family room nucleus of ranch plan

No. 9060—Sliding glass doors admit light and involve indoors with outdoors in the centrally located family room of this sleek ranch style. Placed to invite access from living and sleeping areas, the family room provides informal contrast to the living room, isolated and free from traffic. Tucked between family room and garage, the compact U-shaped kitchen is placed for easy transportation of groceries and has access to basement stairway. Three bedrooms include an ample master bedroom favored with double closets and compartmented bath.

First floor—1,609 sq. ft., Basement—1,609 sq. ft. Garage—572 sq. ft.

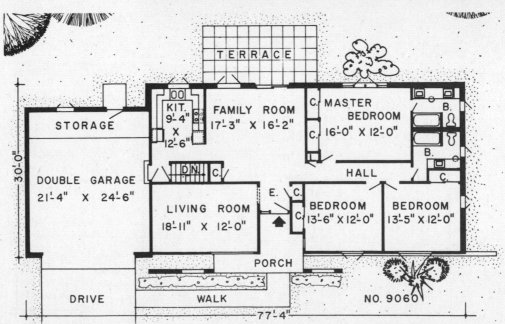

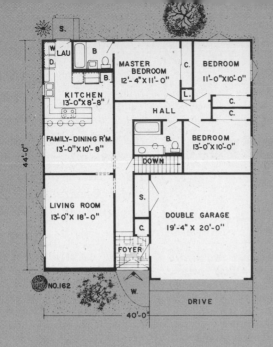

Open family-kitchen area useful

No. 162—Incorporating kitchen, laundry, and family-dining areas into one large, convenient complex helps increase the efficiency of the square footage in this contemporary plan. Tucking the laundry area in an out-of-the-way corner and adding a broom closet and breakfast bar make this area even more useful. For more formal gatherings, a sizable living room, accessible from the foyer, is provided. Long closet and bath benefit the master bedroom, while another bath with built-in vanity serves two more well-closeted bedrooms.

First floor—1,410 sq. ft., Basement—1,373 sq. ft. Garage—406 sq. ft.

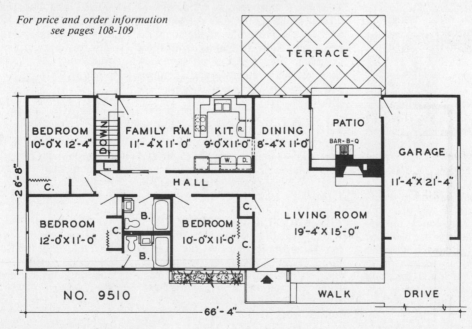

Unique patio . . . Look at it

No. 9510—This design is obviously one for the family with children and lots of family activities. The patio contains a built-in barbecue grill for outdoor cooking. It is enclosed on three sides for protection from the wind. The patio roof is covered with translucent fiberglas panels for maximum natural light. Three bedrooms and two full bathrooms are provided. The family room, kitchen area will be the favorite spot in the house.

First floor—1,343 sq. ft., Basement—1,343 sq. ft. Garage—257 sq. ft.

For price and order information see pages 108-109

The Product Information Source

A wealth of Building Product Information available to you free or at nominal cost. Use the order form on pages 95 & 96 to obtain the literature you want.

Appliances

GROUND FAULTS. Handy guide on how to avoid ground faults in the home that can injure or kill. Describes how ground faults occur and what can be done to make the home safer. New ground fault circuit interrupters eliminate hazard of an appliance grounding and injuring a child or adult. *General Electric. Circle No. 253.*

INFRA-GLOW. Brochure describes Infra-Glow gas·barbeque featuring unique commercial burners which enable the heat to be uniformly distributed over the entire cooking surface. The unit uses less energy, is easier to clean and gives the outdoor char-flavor indoors, without flare-ups. *Vent-A-Hood Co. Circle No. 254.*

VENT-A-HOOD. Brochure package shows complete line of standard and custom range hoods, all with the exclusive fire safe blower system. Both island and wall mount hoods are available in a variety of finishes including baked enamel in many colors, stainless steel and real copper and brass. *Vent-A-Hood Co. Price 50¢. Circle No. 508.*

IN A WORLD OF CLAMOR, COMES A QUIETER DISHWASHER. New dishwashers feature significantly reduced operating sound levels and give consumers the freedom to match the appliance to any kitchen decor. New line includes five built-in and two convertible dishwashers. All models feature three-level wash action and the exclusive Micro-Mesh filter. *Maytag Co. Circle No. 255.*

THERMADOR. Brochures give specifications and photos of complete Thermador line of appliances. *Thermador Waste King, Div. of Norris Ind. Circle No. 102.*

WASTE KING. Brochures give specifications and photos of complete Waste King line of appliances. *Thermador Waste King, Div. of Norris Ind. Circle No. 101.*

KITCHENAID DOES BEAUTIFUL THINGS FOR A KITCHEN. Brochure describes Energy Saver V dishwasher line which heats its own water in every complete cycle and uses less energy, time and water than the previous Energy Saver line. Also covers time-saving trash compactors, disposers, Instant-Hot water dispensers, mixers and coffee mills. *KitchenAid Div., Hobart Corp. Price 50¢. Circle No. 484.*

Bathroom

SAUNA PLANS AND EQUIPMENT SELECTION. Full-color brochure with plans and instructions for installing authentic Finnish saunas. Modular and precut, sauna rooms in sizes from 4'x4' to 8'x12'. Choose one of the standard plans or follow recommendations for designing your own custom sauna. A complete line of quality heaters, controls and accessories. *Amerec Corp. Price 75¢. Circle No. 409.*

THE SAUNA ROOM. Brochure describes the construction and use of your own sauna. Wiring diagrams and floor plans included along with technical data on several models. *Vega Sauna Co. Price 75¢. Circle No. 533.*

TILE SHOWER WATERPROOFING. Asphalt membrane specially designed for waterproofing under tile shower floors. Easy to install and economical. Protects subfloors from water damage from your shower. *Compotite Shower Pan. Circle No. 109.*

BATH CABINETS. Color catalog shows array of charming bath cabinets and ensembles. Decorator models include cabinet equipped with digital clock and night light. Stained-glass model has matching mirror. Bath lighting includes new valances. Winged mirror models in many sizes and finishes. *Nutone. Price $1.00. Circle No. 532.*

OFFICIAL KITCHEN AND BATH COLOR/DESIGN GUIDE. Six kitchen and four bath designs adaptable for use in new homes or remodeling projects are seen in this 64-page, full color guide. *McKone & Co., Inc. Price $4.00. Circle No. 535.*

BATH ACCESSORIES. Full-color folder illustrates Accentware bath accessories, as practical as they are beautiful. Includes dual-track shower bar which lets you dress your tub enclosure with draperies. Switch plates, etc., for use in any room. *Kirsch Co. Circle No. 191.*

BATHE YOURSELF IN QUIET ELEGANCE. No longer is the bathroom the forgotten room in your house. We've created an atmosphere of total comfort and elegance, a pleasant place just for you . . . with softly expressed lines that are pleasing to the eye and with delicate curves that are molded for the contours of your body. Coupled with this grace and comfort is amazing practicality. *Acrylic Tubs Inc. Price 50¢. Circle No. 408.*

EVERYTHING FOR THE BATH. Full-color brochure illustrates full line of lavatories, bathtubs, water closets & whirlpools. You'll find exactly what you're looking for, with color and style to compliment your home. *Briggs, a Jim Walter Co. Circle No. 104.*

WHIRLPOOL BATHS. Full-color catalogue will show you the largest product line in the industry. You can choose from more sizes, shapes, colors and combinations of units than anywhere else. *Jacuzzi® Whirlpool Bath. Circle No. 107.*

Built-ins

VENT-A-VAC. Brochure describes all features of central cleaning systems for the home including layout and installation information. *Vent-A-Hood Co. Circle No. 256.*

THE MASTER SPACE-SAVER. Murphy Beds help to create multi-purpose rooms by providing sleeping accommodations as comfortable as the best standard bed which can also be concealed simply and safely with a minimum of effort. They are not a compromise like a sofa bed and can even be put away fully made up and ready to use. They are easy to conceal because they use a simple and efficient counterbalancing mechanism proven by years of field experience. *Murphy Door Bed Co. Price 50¢. Circle No. 534.*

BUILT-IN IRONING CENTERS. Iron-A-Way by any standard of excellence is the finest ironing center ever built. It has become a household word throughout the United States and provides a compact pressing facility without any storage preparation or putting-a-way problems. When the door is closed, everything is hidden, and it can be painted to match the room or faced with a full-view mirror or other decorative elements. *Iron-A-Way. Circle No. 218.*

CENTRAL CLEANING SYSTEM IN YOUR HOME. New 32 page booklet is off the press. It provides all you need to know about installation and maintenance of a central vacuum cleaning system. Fully illustrated with drawings and photographs. *Wal-Vac Inc. Price 25¢. Circle No. 410.*

Doors & Windows

PLASTIC-VIEW. Heat reflective See-Thru window shades provide outstanding all weather window insulation, plus excellent protection against glare and sun damage to interior furnishings. Plastic-View shades also create daytime privacy whereby insiders can see out but outsiders can't see in . . . the security of a one-way mirror. *Plastic-View Inc. Circle No. 125.*

DOORS OF A LIFETIME. Lifetime Doors manufactures doors of all types including flush hollow or solid core, raised panel, white pine louver/panel and more in finished or unfinished. Color brochure describes and shows all types available. *LifeTime Doors. Circle No. 116.*

VICTORIAN MOULDINGS AND MILLWORK. Unique "turn of the century" mouldings and millwork is available for today's houscs. Includes mouldings, headblocks, baseblocks, casings, wainscoat and baseboard in a standard stock of premium grade pine and oak. Redwood, mahogany and other woods available on custom basis. Catalog illustrates products as well as construction drawings showing the typical uses. *Silverton Victorian Millworks. Price $3.50. Circle No. 509.*

TROCAL RIGID VINYL WINDOWS. 6 page brochure describes double-hung residential windows which combine the energy saving advantages and ruggedness of Trocal commercial windows with the flexibility required for new residential installations or remodeling. *Trocal Window Systems, Div. Dynamit Nobel of America Inc. Circle No. 113.*

INTERNATIONAL DOORS. Brochure describes International Doors from the finest vertical grain Douglas fir or Western Hemlock. Simpson uses original art in the designer series to create solid wood doors with accents. Traditional doors are also featured, and special care is always taken to provide elegance at a realistic price. *Simpson Timber Co. Price 75¢. Circle No. 420.*

ENJOY YOUR HOME MORE WITH A BILCO BASEMENT DOOR. When building your new home, be sure it has this key to a convenient, useful, safe basement . . . a modern, all-steel Bilco Door. It supplements your interior stair. Eliminates unnecessary tracking through first floor rooms. Makes storage easy, convenient. Free folder with sizes, construction data and names of local dealers. *The Bilco Co. Circle No. 121.*

FYPON ENTRANCE SYSTEMS. Brochure features molded millwork for distinctive entrance ways. Moldings, window features specialty millwork, door entrance systems, bow and bay window and roof and shutters. *Fypon Inc. Circle No. 118.*

CUSTOM WINDOW COVERINGS. Ask for our illustrated brochure on custom window coverings. *Ohline Corp. Circle No. 126.*

VICTORIAN RESTORATIONS. 24 page catalog illustrates dozens of solid wood Victorian millwork designs based upon turn-of-the-century originals. Entire line made from kiln dried, premium grade hardwoods. Includes millwork for exterior and interior use. Customizing is available. *Cumberland Woodcraft Co., Inc. Price $3.00. Circle No. 418.*

The Product Information Source

GUIDE TO ENERGY-SAVING WINDOWS.
16 page booklet includes the components that comprise a quality window; various styles of windows, proper window locations for optimum light, ventilation, and fuel savings; condensation and the effect quality windows can have on energy usage. *National Woodwork Mfg. Assoc. Circle No. 209.*

BOX BAY WINDOW.
A new 90-degree box bay window has been added to Andersen's line of quality windows and gliding patio doors. Features Perma-Shield casement windows with low-maintenance features of double-pane insulating glass and vinyl-sheathing over preservative-treated wood core sash and frame. *Andersen Corp. Circle No. 257.*

NATURAL BEAUTY AND INSULATING.
16-page color catalog covers complete line of woven wood shades, draperies and folding doors. Emphasizes overall theme of natural beauty and natural insulating quality of wood. Also offer better light, ventilation and efficiency. Includes product applications and specifications, plus a description of how the products are manufactured. *Aeroshade, Inc. Circle No. 258.*

COMPLETE OUTSIDE BASEMENT ENTRANCE!
You probably know the sales appeal direct basement access gives your home. Perm-Entry makes it easy and economical for you to include it in your home. The concrete stairwell is manufactured and installed to rigid specifications, and capped with the rugged watertight heavy gauge steel PermEntry door. *Perm Entry Co. Circle No. 122.*

HOW TO INSTALL INTERIOR JAMBS AND EXTERIOR DOOR FRAMES.
8-page brochure for do-it-yourselfers explaining the differences between interior jambs (both flat and adjustable) and exterior frames, plan-ning requirements, tools and supplies needed, step-by-step installation procedure illustrations, plus much more. *Wood Moulding & Millwork Producers. Price 40¢. Circle No. 491.*

GARAGE DOORS FOR EYE APPEALING STYLE.
Colorful booklet shows variety of garage doors to enhance the appearance of your home. How to instructions includes helpful hints on installing automatic door openers. *Raynor Manufacturing Co. Price 50¢. Circle No. 536.*

WORLD'S LARGEST DOOR CATALOG.
Unique 68 page full-color catalog packed with over 1000 hard-to-find quality millwork items. Entry doors, French, sash and interior doors, bifolds, patio doors, energy saving door systems, screen doors, spindles, stair parts, columns, posts. Of special note: leaded glass and laser carved doors. *E. A. Nord Co. Price $2.50. Circle No. 510.*

Fireplaces & Stoves

WOOD SPLITTING MADE EASIER.
Literature tells of unique axe which splits many woods in a single stroke. Chopper 1™ possesses rotating levers which transform the downward stroke to a powerful outward force and also prevents the axe from sticking in the wood making the splitting of firewood faster and easier than ever before. *Chopper Industries. Circle No. 128.*

WOODMASTER PRIMER.
Descriptive pamphlet showing savings on home heating costs by burning wood as opposed to oil and electricity, with charts showing the heating values of wood and savings in dollars on wood versus oil/electricity. *Suburban Mfg. Co. Circle No. 259.*

CUSTOM FIREPLACE ENCLOSURES.
8-Page brochure and price sheet describes our custom glass fireplace enclosures. Each unit is individually constructed from your measurements or our template. *The Iron Shop. Circle No. 260.*

ULTIMATE IN FIREPLACE EFFICIENCY.
Colorful brochure describes the operation of fireplace inserts. Provides illustrated details of air flow, installation, and dimensions, and features the WOODMASTER Fireplace Insert and Deluxe Fireplace Insert along with specifications of each. *Suburban Mfg. Co. Circle No. 261.*

WOOD BURNING FIREPLACES.
Full color performance report and do-it-yourself installation planner brochures on Majestic's most efficient fireplace — Warm Majic, rated 41-43% efficient by Wood Heating Alliance. Fireplace available with outside air and glass enclosure kits. *Majestic. Price $1.00. Circle No. 511.*

WOOD MANTELS GIVE OLD FIREPLACES NEW LIFE.
Hand-crafted wood mantels offer the professional builder, remodler or homeowner-handyman, an economical and easy way to add new life and looks to any fireplace. *Readybuilt. Circle No. 227.*

FIREPLACE STOVES.
Full color detailed brochure tells about discovering heating with wood and coal in comfort and style with a multi-fuel Comforter. Quality, efficiency, and beautiful fire-viewing are the outstanding features of this classic 24-hour burning cast-iron heater. *Comforter Stove Works. Price $1.00. Circle No. 476.*

EASY LOG LIGHTING.
Blue Flame log lighting system makes heating with modern pre-fab fireplaces more energy efficient by using less than 1¢ of natural gas to quickly ignite a roaring log or coal blaze. System is easily installed in either pre-fab or existing masonry fireplaces. Saves oil, gas and electricity in home heating. *Canterbury Enterprises. Circle No. 133.*

WOOD & COAL/WOOD BURNING CIRCULATORS.
King circulators are airtight for long intervals between fueling and include automatic temperature control for even heating for up to 12 hours on one load of fuel. Attractive styling. King heaters move heated air naturally and offer cooler outside cabinet temperatures. *Martin Ind. Price 25¢. Circle No. 492.*

ASHLEY WOOD BURNING CENTRAL FURNACE.
Engineered for installation as a supplementary furnace to existing oil or gas central systems or as a totally independent central furnace. Allows up to 12 hours on one load of wood. *Martin Ind. Price 15¢. Circle No. 493.*

FIREPLACES & MORE FIREPLACES.
Literature displays full line of fireplaces. There's one to suit every decor from the ultra modern to the rustic Early American. Complete with energy saving and decorating ideas. *Malm Fireplaces Inc. Circle No. 127.*

FIREPLACE INSERTS.
The latest in fireplace inserts deliver both high heat output and high efficiency. Unique design offers see-through glass doors for viewing the beauty of the fire — and interchangeable air-tight doors for extend-

ed burn times. Product is UL tested and listed. Includes dual variable-speed internal blowers for flush-face installation *Thermograte Inc. Circle No. 216.*

Floors & Walls

TESSITURA II. 25 real fabric wall-coverings in 87 colorways on the exclusive "Tessitura" ground. 4 companion fabrics in 15 colorways also available. *James Seeman Studios, Div. of Masonite Corp. Circle No. 262.*

THIS GOOD EARTH II. Collection of wallcoverings and companion fabrics inspired by natural elements from all over the world. 26 wallcovering designs in 100 colorways are shown with the 8 fabrics in 34 colorways. *James Seeman Studios, Div. of Masonite Corp. Circle No. 263.*

THE TOP FLOOR SINCE 1898. Parquet and plank flooring. Full-color booklet illustrates a full line of parquet block and plank flooring. The many patterns come unfinished and prefinished. Booklet includes specification chart. *Harris Mfg. Co. Price $1.00. Circle No. 516.*

PLAQUES, TABLEAUX, & TILES. Set of 3 booklets illustrating the Authentic OLD DUTCH HAND PAINTED DELFT tiles, tableaux and ceramic relief plaques. The individual tiles are stocked in blue crackled and non-crackled, and POLYCHROME crackled, as well as tableaux in POLYCHROME crackled. *Amsterdam Corp. Price $2.50. Circle No. 517.*

BEAUTIFUL WALLS & FLOORS. Full color brochure highlights the entire Z-BRICK product line, including decorative facing brick and stone, flooring products, RUFF-IT Acrylic Sculpture Coat and All-Weather Stucco. *Z-BRICK Co. Circle No. 280.*

CARPET FOUNDATION. Densified prime urethane foam used under wall to wall carpeting and also under your most prized area rugs. Material includes two brochures. One explains the benefits of OMALON and the other is a practical Room Planner/Decorating Kit to help you plan your room settings around your lifestyle. *Olin Corp. Circle No. 264.*

THE PANELING BOOK. 28 page booklet includes how-to instructions, diagrams, and full-color photos of rooms you'll want to duplicate. Make this your complete guide to paneling any room, whether building or remodeling your home. *Georgia-Pacific. Price $1.00. Circle No. 429.*

SUPERIOR INTERIORS. Handsome, new full-color brochure showing unique decorating ideas using red cedar shingles or handsplit shakes on interiors. See how these products bring fascinating texture and color into a room. "How to apply" information shown. *Red Cedar Shingle & Handsplit Shake Bureau. Price 35¢. Circle No. 451.*

NATURESCAPES. Brochure offers an exciting design alternative for residential or commercial decor. Naturescapes photomurals are durable, dry-strippable, and meet all institutional standards. *Naturescapes, Inc. Price $1.00. Circle No. 431.*

HOW TO WATERPROOF MASONRY WALLS. A 16-page illustrated booklet that explains the common causes of seepage and suggests techniques and products for treating interior and exterior masonry surfaces to withstand moisture penetration. *United Gilsonite Laboratories. Price 25¢. Circle No. 456.*

THE PETITE LOOK, THE PREFERRED LOOK, AND KITCHENS AND BATHS. 3 brochures featuring small prints, the pattern look, and ideas for your kitchen and bath. *Panta Astor Wallcovering. Circle No. 225.*

SHINE-EASE NO-WAX FLOOR. Full-color booklet describes the ease of installing and maintaining a beautiful floor with the use of Azrock floor tile. Shine-ease offers you easy living extras at a most affordable price. *Azrock Floor Products. Circle No. 143.*

ALTERNATIVE FLOORING. Brochure illustrates the use of ceramic floor tile. Tile that is durable enough for floors and yet light enough to use with coordinating walls. *Marazzi USA Inc. Circle No. 139.*

ULTIMATE IN HARDWOOD FLOORING. Brochure presents the complete product line, from the custom classics and end grain floors to basic plank and parquet. Line is directed toward the upper-end specifier and consumer for that special residential accent area. *Kentucky Wood Floors Inc. Price $1.00. Circle No. 428.*

DECORATIVE STONE. Brochure describes manufactured building stone veneer made from lightweight concrete. Although available at a fraction of the cost of natural stone, it is hard to distinguish from the real thing. The light weight permits easy installation over nearly any existing or new surface. *Eldorado Stone Corp. Circle No. 138.*

ASTOR WALLCOVERING. The answer to the important questions in wallcovering are answered in this full-color 16 page booklet. *Panta Astor Wallcovering. Circle No. 224.*

GENUINE HARDWOOD FLOORS. Full-color brochures detail beautiful Applachian Oak parquet flooring. Elegance has never been so practical. *Pennwood. Circle No. 145.*

NEW LOOK. Brochure describes how you can give your home a New Look with lustrous hardwood parquet floors. Your parquet floors will be a conversation piece and the envy of those around you. *Peace Flooring Co., Inc. Circle No. 137.*

DOVETAIL COLLECTION. A color brochure of ornamental plaster. Molding, cornices, ceiling medallions, and complete decorative ceilings are included. A classic and beautiful addition to any home and easy to install. *Dovetail, Inc. Price $1.00. Circle No. 512.*

REDWOOD PANELING. Available in a wide choice of patterns, grades, sizes and textures, redwood offers a rich natural complement to walls, ceilings, and accent areas. It's a natural insulator against both heat and cold. *Simpson Timber Co. Price 50¢. Circle No. 513.*

HOW TO WATERPROOF YOUR HOME. A fold-out brochure features schematic drawings of the exterior of a house and an inside basement wall with concrete and masonry trouble spots pinpointed. It includes a special section on how to correct damp basement walls. *Thoro System Prod. Price 10¢. Circle No. 515.*

Furniture & Furnishing

SHELVING. Series of full-color folders explains and shows three shelving styles, one wall-hung and two freestanding twist togethers. Special units for stereo equipment. Designed and finished to look like expensive furniture, but the cost is less. *Kirsch Co. Circle No. 192.*

CLASSIC CHAIRS . . . AND MORE. 16-page, full color catalog illustrating a large variety of classic imported chairs and tables, both contemporary and traditional, of wood, chrome, leather, wicker, marble and glass. *Intrends Int., Div. of Walker & Zanger, Inc. Price $2.00. Circle No. 495.*

ELEGANT SHEEPSKIN & LAMBSKIN RUGS. This color brochure describes the beauty, warmth and durability of a variety of luxuriously soft wool sheep and lambskin rugs, the ultimate in dynamic decorating. A special offer on these exceptional New Zealand woolskins is made possible through a limited shipment. New Zealand produces some of the highest quality wool anywhere due to the moderate climate. In most wool producing regions of the world, the cold winters will produce brittle areas in the wool fiber, causing these fibers to gradually break and making the fleece thinner. This doesn't happen to New Zealand wool. New Zealand care has converted one of nature's most versatile resources into fine prestigious furnishing rugs to add distinction and elegance to any home. Find out how you too can own one of these most delightful decorator pieces. *Treasures. Circle No. 210.*

TABLE TOPS. Literature shows table tops that are geared for end use such as dining room tables, dinettes, coffee tables, end tables, or counter tops where the physical properties of our material, which is called Radwood, can offer styling and design ideal for the residential or contract market. *Radiation Technology, Inc. Circle No. 146.*

OLD SOUTH REPRODUCTIONS OFFERS A RETURN TO ELEGANCE. Classic and timely styling from bygone days, masterfully recreated for today. Cast aluminum tables, chairs, settees, coat rack, umbrella stands . . . hundreds of singularly distinctive pieces for home and patio. Full-color catalog depicts wide range of items in lovely finishes. *Moultrie Mfg. Co. Price $1.00. Circle No. 460.*

FURNITURE. Now you've finished your home you want furniture to complete the picture. Catalog gives hundreds of decorating ideas and shows the complete line of furnishings for every room in your home. *Terra Furniture Inc. Price $5.00. Circle No. 537.*

UNIQUE COPPER FURNISHINGS IN EASILY ASSEMBLED KITS. Modern home furnishings are available in knock down kits that can be assembled by anyone in under one hour. The beauty and clean lines of these copper and glass items work well in any contemporary or American traditional setting. *Copper Concepts. Circle No. 228.*

Hardware

BRASS RAIL & FITTINGS. Bar foot rails, hand rails, brass "fencing," custom bends, tubing and fittings to build about anything from brass beds to glass racks. *Ship'N Out, Inc. Circle No. 275.*

DISTINCTIVE TOUCH OF CLASS. Catalog of unusual, hard-to-find hardware, plumbing, and lighting fixtures. Quality reproductions are made from solid brass, porcelain, oak and wrought iron. Complement 18th and 19th century decors as well as contemporary homes. *Renovator's Supply, Inc. Price $2.00. Circle No. 519.*

GARAGE DOORS & OPENERS. Frantz has the best of both, shown in full color in two new catalogs. Model homes and driveway designs help in home planning. Opener is state-of-the-art model — new programmable design with top safety features. *Frantz Mfg. Co. Price 75¢. Circle No. 518.*

SOLUTIONS TO BARRIER-FREE DOOR CONTROL. 16 page, full color brochure explains the problems caused by barriers to handicapped individuals and offers methods to effectively meet the demands for barrier-free environments and cost-effective implementation. *Reading-Dorma Closer Corp. Circle No. 250.*

RELIABLE SIMPLICITY IN DOOR CONTROLS. Reading-Dorma Closer Corp., has published a unique 16 page product guide to hydraulic door controls. The comprehensive catalog features an easy-to-read guide to ANSI numbers, and has a cross index to comparable competitive products. In addition, there is a Typical Application section that lists the correct product to use for a particular application. *Reading-Dorma Closer Corp. Circle No. 114.*

DECORATIVE HARDWARE. 32 page decorating booklet shows how to select and install hardware items to coordinate each room with matching style door locks, bath hardware, cabinet hardware, and wall switch plates. Several designer hardware styles are detailed. *Amerock Corp. Price 25¢. Circle No. 433.*

HANDCRAFTED HARDWARE OF THE COLONIES. For over a third of a century, Acorn has been reproducing the charm and warmth of Early American Hardware. Booklet shows full line of antique looking hardware for your home. Beautiful yet sturdy and practical. *Acorn Manufacturing Co., Inc. Price $3.00. Circle No. 504.*

Heating & Cooling

THE ENERGY SAVERS. Tabloid describes summer related energy saving products including air conditioner and cooling air deflectors. *Deflecto Corp. Circle No. 149.*

HOW TO GET THE MOST FROM YOUR COMFORT INVESTMENT. 16 page booklet explains the importance of clean air, humidity and air circulation to your comfort system. Includes sections on solar heating and efficient two-speed cooling. Plus tips on saving energy. *Lennox Industries, Inc. Circle No. 229.*

SAVANNAH. The Savannah ceiling fan features traditional elegance and modern American engineering. 38'' or 42'' blades. Flexible blade hub, vibration absorbing motor mounts and a heavy duty sealed ball-bearing induction-type motor for reliable, quiet operation. Also features solid state variable speed control and motor reversing switch. *Old Jacksonville Ceiling Fans, Nichols-Kusan, Inc. Circle No. 266.*

HEIRLOOM DELUXE. New 42 inch Heirloom Deluxe features reversible operation, a variety of blade colors in stencil or cane insert, a 7 year warranty and three speed pull chain operation. Available in Bright Brass, Antique Brass, and Antique Copper. Price is FAN-TASTIC! *Moss Mfg. Circle No. 267.*

ENERGY SAVINGS WITH NATURAL VENTILATION. Bulletin describes how whole house ventilation system can be used for summer comfort and energy savings by reducing air conditioning. Details advantages and describes the solid state speed control and timer control features. Installs in any home. *Kool-O-Matic Corp. Price 25¢. Circle No. 435.*

HUNTER CEILING FANS. 20-page brochure includes 22 cast iron motors, 32 wood blades and over 100 distinctive accessories for residential, commercial, and industrial use. Limited lifetime warranty. *Robbins & Myers, Inc. Price $1.00. Circle No. 520.*

ECONOMICAL HEAT WITH HOT WATER COMFORT. Booklet describes Softheat hot water baseboard system that, in most cases, costs less than kerosene to operate while providing wonderful, automatic comfort with safety and convenience. For one room or entire home. *Intertherm, Inc. Price 25¢. Circle No. 521.*

AIR CIRCULATOR GRILLE. Redistributes air to make temperature more uniform. Utilizes electric fan to draw warm air or cool air from one room and redirect it into another level of the same room or to an adjoining room. Saves money on utility bills and operates on mere pennies a day. *Hutch Mfg. Circle No. 265.*

AIR MOVER GRILLE. Moves warm or cool air where it is needed. The economical alternative to revamping a central heating or cooling system which fails to maintain uniform temperatures in adjoining rooms or between floors. *Hutch Mfg. Circle No. 281.*

KEEP IT MOVING. Lomanco describes how to keep air moving with their complete line of ventilation products. Includes whole-house central fans, turbine ventilators, ridge line ventilators and power ventilators. *Lomanco, Inc. Circle No. 231.*

EASY INSTALLATION. Brochures describe whole house attic fans that are designed to cool a house at great energy savings and are a breeze to install by the average do-it-yourselfer. *Emerson Environmental Prod. Circle No. 232.*

AIR CLEANING. Booklet describes air cleaning and presents efficiency data on common household pollutants and how to control them with a new type air cleaner. *Research Products Corp. Circle No. 152.*

CARRIER'S WEATHERMASTER III. Literature describes the only heat pump system on the market which houses the compressor and all critical controls out of the weather. Compressor and controls are installed in garage, utility room or basement, meaning improved system reliability as critical components are protected from rain, snow and freezing temeratures. Concept, system operation, features, accessories, physical data and dimensions, and performance data all included. *Carrier Corp. Circle No. 194.*

HUMIDIFICATION. Booklet discusses relative humidity and lists several points to consider when purchasing a humidifier. *Research Products Corp. Circle No. 151.*

CARRIER. The Carrier line of upflow gas-fired furnaces, featuring solid-state controls, low noise levels and high operating efficiency, consists of both standing pilot (58GS) and electronic ignition (58GP) models. Literature describes full line, options (including flue damper), solid-state control systems, features, accessories, physical dimensions, selection procedures, performance and application data, and depicts typical installations. *Carrier Corp. Circle No. 196.*

THE HOT SHOT. Carrier's heat reclaim device for domestic hot water systems, automatically recycles heat energy from a residential air conditioner or heat pump system to a home's hot water system. Results in reduced domestic hot water energy consumption costs. Literature describes concept, operation, dimensions and connections, and typical piping and wiring arrangements. *Carrier Corp. Circle No. 195.*

Home Plan Books

COMPLETE HOME PLANS COLLECTION. This 10-book library comes complete with a handsome plastic binder. Packed with more than 750 different home designs (many in full color), this collection will be the one and only source you'll need to find that special home. There are hundreds of designs of all sizes, styles, and configurations imaginable, and low-cost construction drawings with energy-saving features are available for each one. If you are serious about a new home, then this collection is a must. *Garlinghouse. Price $19.50. Circle No. 505.*

DUPLEX, CONDOMINIUM AND MULTI-UNIT HOME PLANS. The Garlinghouse Company has consolidated their multi-unit designs into one source. You'll find over fifty designs suitable for residential or resort settings including ranch, Tudor, Swiss and Spanish designs. Includes duplexes, triplexes, fourplexes and larger. *Garlinghouse. Price $3.50. Circle No. 530.*

TRADITIONAL HOME PLANS. Over 125 traditional designs, many with solar energy features, are found in this book from the Garlinghouse Company. English Tudor, Cape Cod, Victorian, Oriental and Classic Farmhouse are just several of the styles. Many full-color illustrations and easy to read floor plans. *Garlinghouse. Price $3.50. Circle No. 531.*

The Product Information Source

SINGLE-LEVEL AND UNDERGROUND HOME PLANS. This book from the Garlinghouse Company provides you with over 130 new home plan designs to aid you in choosing and planning the perfect home. Energy efficient underground and bermed homes are two of the special features in this book. Low-cost construction drawings are available for all designs. *Garlinghouse. Price $3.50. Circle No. 538.*

MULTI-LEVEL AND SOLAR HOME PLANS. The latest in energy-saving designs and solar use are just two of the many unique features in this new book of over 120 home plan designs (many in full color). You are sure to find the home to fit your individual preferences in this comprehensive collection of truly great designs. *Garlinghouse. Price $3.50. Circle No. 539.*

Kitchens & Cabinets

CABINETS. Beautifully designed contemporary door styles accent today's modern kitchens. Birchcraft's fine assortment of stylish patterns allows you to choose the perfect door to fit your personal tastes as well as the wood and stain finish that best compliments your overall design. Ranging from sleek, ultra-modern to country casual, the Birchcraft line of contemporary cabinet styles is sure to compliment the most epicurean tastes. *Birchcraft Kitchens. Circle No. 154.*

KITCHEN AND LAUNDRY DESIGNS FOR THE '80s. Helping plan kitchens and laundries that are both energy efficient and attractive is Maytag's idea in this booklet. Included are floor plans and ideas on selection and use of home appliances to maximize energy conservation in the home, plus an energy audit that you can use to rate the energy efficiency of your home. *Maytag Co. Circle No. 235.*

SPACE BUILDER. Ventilated shelving by Closet Maid is the modern method of solving storage space problems quickly and easily. Creates additional storage space without remodeling in bedroom closets. Can turn a blank wall into a pantry in kitchens. Keeps cleaning supplies high and dry in utility rooms. *Closet Maid. Circle No. 234.*

ELKAY BOOKLET OF KITCHEN IDEAS. Elkay stainless steel sinks and other products give a smart contemporary look that flatters any interior, blends with every color scheme. Work-saving accessories in many models and sizes. Easy cleaning . . . longer wear! *Elkay Mfg. Co. Price 50¢. Circle No. 522.*

KITCHEN & BATH PLANNING GUIDE. This 16-page color booklet contains helpful suggestions on how homeowners can get the "dream kitchen" or bath of their choice. It covers subjects such as efficient "work triangles," where to get professional help, and a consumer guide to cabinet selection. *National Kitchen Cabinet Assoc. Price 50¢. Circle No. 540.*

NEWEST IN STORAGE. Literature describes a unique new furniture storage system that is scheduled to be offered nationally when the franchise network is completed. The system is designed and manufactured in Europe, where storage space is a real problem. It is iP20's simplicity and flexibility that makes it so attractive. The shelves, drawers, cabinets and accessories are easily set up with only a screwdriver. *iP20. Circle No. 156.*

KITCHEN SINKS. Complete catalog gives specifications and photos of a complete line of stainless kitchen sinks. *Polar Ware Co. Price 25¢. Circle No. 403.*

EXCLUSIVE KITCHENS. This four-page color brochure tells you how to color coordinate and decorate your kitchen. Exclusive electic decorator series allows you to color coordinate your kitchen in 999 electrifying styles. See the unlimited design possibilities in kitchen cabinets. *Rich Maid Kitchens, Inc. Price 30¢. Circle No. 440.*

PUSH BUTTON PLUMBING. Booklet details Ultraflo, a system which conserves both water and energy and can be installed quickly at much less cost than conventional plumbing. Reduces the water bill up to 35% and saves about 25% on the heating of water. *Ultraflo Corp. Circle No. 110.*

SPECIFICATIONS AND ACCESSORIES GUIDE. The literature contains diagrams and dimensions for all units, and shows Haas' wide array of accessories and specialty cabinets. Complete specifications and a color page of the full line of storage accessories are also included. *Haas Cabinet Co. Circle No. 208.*

SOLID COLOR COLLECTION. Illustrating the 64 top decorative colors of the decorative laminate. *Wilsonart. Price 50¢. Circle No. 502.*

THE CENTER OF FAMILY LIVING. New four color packet, while showing cabinet styles of oak, pine, pecan and maple, provides necessary and helpful information on kitchen design and layout as well as decorating ideas. Matching bathroom cabinetry, hutches and wall systems provide added storage ideas for every room of your home. *Arist-O-Kraft. Price $1.00. Circle No. 444.*

KITCHEN CABINETS. Wood-Hu Kitchens is a custom manufacturer of all wood kitchen cabinets. Color brochure describes variety of cabinets all designed with todays fashion in mind. Showing 32 different door styles. *Wood-Hu Kitchens, Inc. Price 50¢. Circle No. 443.*

KITCHEN UNIT WITH MICROWAVE OVEN. For the first time, a microwave oven is available with a 30" kitchen unit in one factory-assembled unit. Materials describe further details. *King Refrigerator Corp. Price 25¢. Circle No. 486.*

LIVING CENTER. Distinctive kitchens designed for the living patterns of your family are shown in full-color booklet. Planning procedures to use space wisely for well-organized step saving work areas are discussed thoroughly. *Kitchen Kompact Inc. Price $3.00. Circle No. 445.*

Lighting

NATURAL SKYLIGHTS. Send for this full-color brochure describing standard size sky-light models. Includes photographs of room interiors and the names of dealers in your area. *Naturalite, Inc. Circle No. 160.*

A TOUCH OF CLASS. Liviton's Decora line of rocket switches, available in all home harmonizing colors are indeed a decorative touch in a home that adds "class." Dimmers, both of the wall variety and table top, are also important effects. Even dimmers that are touch sensitive, has a memory and has a true decorator look. *Leviton Manufacturing Co., Inc. Circle No. 162.*

HOME CONTROL SYSTEM. From Leviton, a modular remote control plug in system which permits the user to control up to 16 lights or appliances from one location in addition to convenience a dimming feature provides energy savings. A single button for all lights, off or on, also has the advantage of security. Starter kit includes control box and 2 modules. *Leviton Mfg. Co., Inc. Circle No. 213.*

ARCHITECTURAL LANTERNS. Trimble House architectural lanterns feature colonial, victorian and contemporary styling to harmonize perfectly with buildings and landscape new and old. All lanterns are totally cast in aluminum offering maintenance free, functional construction with enduring elegance of design. *Trimblehouse Corp. Circle No. 161.*

Patio & Yard

STORAGE BUILDINGS. Literature shows a complete line of galvanized steel and aluminum storage buildings. The styles include gable, high gable, gambrel and high gambrel in various sizes and colors. They also have a line of aspenite buildings; all factory cut and drilled. Easy assembly. *Arrow Group Industries. Circle No. 181.*

REDWOOD, HOT WATER & YOU: A PERFECT MIXTURE. A colorful brochure describing the joys of owning your own hot tub. Gordon & Grant redwood hot tubs are individually hand-crafted by highly skilled coopers from carefully selected clear all-heart kiln-dried vertical grain redwood. Every tub is an individual. *Gordon & Grant. Circle No. 189.*

ORNAMENTAL GATES & FENCES. Color catalog illustrates a selection of ornamental gates and panels for fencing. Master plan illustrates how to design a brick wall containing ornamental fence panels. Catalog also includes complete line of outdoor furniture for poolside, fountains, urns, planters, garden plaques and mailboxes as well as a variety of small gift items. *Moultrie Mfg. Co. Price $1.00. Circle No. 447.*

FOUNTAINS & WATERFALLS. Full-color literature shows the beauty of nature's sparkling streams and the serenity of her still waters in lightweight fiberglass creations. Easy to install and affordable. These products will transform their surroundings into fascinating garden areas-places to relax and escape from the tensions of the day. *Hermitage Gardens. Price $1.00. Circle No. 446.*

DECKS ADD FUN & VALUE. This year enjoy your home inside and out by investing in contemporary outdoor living. Redwood Design-a-Deck Plans Kit can help you get started. As with any project, careful advance planning assures more efficient deck construction. This kit helps minimize confusion by giving you everything you need to know, including materials lists, information on which redwood grades to use and where, which finishes to apply and how. Nails and fastening systems, as well as pre-cut deck patterns, 20-page instruction manual and planning grid. *California Redwood Assoc. Price $5.00. Circle No. 541.*

REDWOOD FOR OUTDOOR USE. New brochure features a wide variety of outdoor uses for which redwood excels — decks, patios, fences, sunscreens. *Simpson Timber Co. Price 75¢. Circle No. 523.*

GARDEN SETTINGS. New eight-page color booklet, Redwood Garden Settings for Spas, Tubs, Pools, features spectacular idea-starting hot tub surrounds, poolside decks and spa shelters, all using the economical redwood garden grades. Design and planning tips can help you built a luxury redwood retreat in your own backyard. *California Redwood Assoc. Price 50¢. Circle No. 475.*

UNDERGROUND SPRINKLERS. Brochure shows how to install Rain Jet permanent underground sprinkler system with a minimum of sprinkler heads and digging. Patented nozzles distribute rain-like droplets evenly. Choice of heads includes squares, strips, circles, etc. Flexible pipe and full flow fittings make installation easy. *Rain Jet Corporation. Price 50¢. Circle No. 466.*

WHIRLPOOL SPAS. Full-color catalogue shows the full range of spas available with detailed design. *Jacuzzi® Whirlpool Bath. Circle No. 108.*

The Product Information Source

SHOWERS OF DIAMONDS. Fountains by Rain Jet. Sculptured patterns from rotating fountain head provides arresting beauty. Alive! Vital! Fascinating! Lights and color blender available for jewel-like effects. Water recirculates. Complete fountain bowls to 8 feet. Full color catalog. *Rain Jet Corp. Price 50¢. Circle No. 465.*

Roofing

A HOMEOWNER'S GUIDE TO QUALITY ROOFING. When to replace an existing roof, should you do the job yourself, how to pick a contractor and a review of general roofing procedures are discussed in this brochure. Also discusses the features of asphalt shingles and illustrates the latest styles and colors. Contains a color guide to help coordinate roofing with siding and trim. Plus a section on talking the roofer's language and tips on the care of roofs. *Asphalt Roofing Mfg. Price 35¢. Circle No. 498.*

OVER-ROOF WITH CEDAR. Color brochure showing how home owners can save applying a beautiful cedar shingle or shake roof right over their old roof. Detailed "how to" information plus data on tools and techniques. *Red Cedar Shingle & Handsplit Shake Bureau. Price 10¢. Circle No. 448.*

REMODELING IDEAS. New color brochure packed with ideas on how to remodel with red cedar shingles and handsplit shakes. Photographs show remarkable step-by-step transformation of homes. Projects from simple over-roofing to major remodeling. *Red Cedar Shingle & Handsplit Shake Bureau. Price 25¢. Circle No. 450.*

HOW TO DO IT . . . AND SAVE. Color brochure featuring economy grade red cedar shingles and Handsplit shakes. Filled with ideas on the use of #2, #3 and #4 shingles plus #2 shakes on walls, planters, furniture and in many other ways around the home. *Red Cedar Shingle & Handsplit Shake Bureau. Price 10¢. Circle No. 449.*

ROOFING MAGAZINE TELLS ALL. 8-page magazine filled with helpful tips on everything from selecting the right color roof for your home to thoughts on roofing and energy savings. *CertainTeed Corp. Circle No. 236.*

Security

IN-THE-FLOOR-SAFE. A revolutionary, low cost, In-The-Floor-Safe has been developed by Meilink Safe Company. This new unit comes in a key lock version or a key and combination version. Capacity is 1188 cubic inches. *Meilink Safe Co. Circle No. 279.*

SUPER SECURITY. Latch-Gard II, a security device for homes, apartments, motels and hotels, offers real security. A door can be opened safely one inch to view the would-be intruder. The super tough aircraft cable cannot be violated as easily as the common chair door guard. *Latch-Gard, Inc. Price 25¢. Circle No. 543.*

KEYLESS ENTRY. Pushbutton combination door locks. Press a four digit combination from the outside and door unlocks automatically. 10,000 possible combinations. Mechanically activated, no electricity. Interior unlocks by pressing a button. With bilt-in nitelatch, 1" throw deadbolt defies forcible entry. No keys to lose or misplace. Guaranteed pickproof! *Preso-Matic Lock Co. Circle No. 177.*

Solar

HEATING. Booklet titled "Solar Energy Facts" contains background information, detailed descriptions of all current types of solar heating units, as well as their practical applications. A

special point of emphasis is given to the economies of solar heating in today's economy. *Research Products Corp. Circle No. 268.*

ONE DESIGN WATERWALL. Completely packaged solar system. One screw secures the child-proof furnace between studs, rafters or floor joists. Fill them with tap water, cap them, and the sun does the rest. The decorator trim possibilities are endless. Think of them as old fashioned radiators — without the fuel bill. *One Design. Circle No. 269.*

SOLAR HEATING. Literature describes a series of components for solar and radiant heating that are highly durable and low in cost. The versatile, flexible material of Tube Mat components makes the systems ideal for retrofit applications, and they integrate neatly into new construction. In addition they have developed a whole new solar technology which is extremely easy to install. *Bio-Energy Systems, Inc. Circle No. 277.*

SOLAR & RADIANT HEATING SYSTEMS. The versatile, flexible material of Tube Mat components make our systems ideal for retrofit applications, and they integrate neatly into new construction. Easy to install. *Bio-Energy Systems, Inc. Circle No. 278.*

AMETEK POWER SYSTEMS DIVISION. Currently offering its Sunjammer Solar collectors to qualified contractors and builders for installation in residential space and hot water heating systems. The product incorporates an aluminum extruded housing finished with the Sherwin-Williams PowerClad® baked enamel paint finish, high transmission solar glazing, and all copper absorber plate using black chrome selective coating. 20, 26, and 33 square feet sizes available. *Ametek Power Systems Division. Circle No. 188.*

SOLAR HOME SYSTEMS. Brochure describes the workings of Solar Energy and how you can use it to heat your home in winter and cool it in summer. *Solara Technical Center. Circle No. 169.*

HOT WATER THE SOLAR WAY. Full-color brochure describes economical approach to domestic hot water also shows pre-plumbed tanks that are used with the collector to form the main components of a Solar D.H.W. System. *Solar Warehouse, Distributors for Jet Air Solar Products. Circle No. 167.*

SOLARMATE HOT WATER SYSTEMS. 6-page brochure describes the quality line of efficient and dependable solar hot water systems. *Lennox Ind., Inc. Circle No. 242.*

SOLAR COLLECTOR INCREASES BTU EFFICIENCY. Brochure describes breakthrough in solar collector design and manufacture enabling a significant boost in BTU's per dollar. Two exceptionally light models are available including a double glazed acrylic-Teflon collector. *Sunearth Solar Products Corp. Circle No. 164.*

SOLAR SHINGLE. Full color brochure describes the solar shingle, a unique approach to the solar collector. The shingles provide a dual service as solar collectors and as a roofing material which can be used to heat your pool, spa or hot tub. They are aesthetically pleasing while maintaining thermal efficiency. *Jet Air, Inc. Circle No. 239.*

SOLAR COLLECTORS. Features flat plate copper collectors for use in domestic hot water and space heating. Designed to be efficient, yet economical while having an anticipated life span of 20 years or more. *National Solar Supply. Circle No. 241.*

V-12 SOLAR COLLECTOR. Heat With The Sun! Save our vital resources while you save on your monthly utility bills. "Daytime Assist" and "Complete—With Storage" solar systems available. Brochure describes solar collectors that heat your home and water. *Sunflower Energy Works, Inc. Circle No. 240.*

THE ACROSUN COLLECTOR. The AcroSun collector is a well constructed all copper collector with glass plate, aluminum anodized housing, aluminum backing and is fully insulated. It is available in Flat Black Paint or Black Chrome. *AcroSun Industries Inc. Circle No. 182.*

LET THE SUN WORK FOR YOU. Literature describes complete line of solar heating equipment for domestic, commercial and industrial applications, consisting of solar collectors, universal mounting frame and automatic temperature control system. *Solar-Eye Products, Inc. Circle No. 185.*

Specialties

REDWOOD INTERIOR/EXTERIOR GUIDE. Highlights top-quality exterior siding and interior paneling in 8 pages. Applications and techniques for building with the many grades and patterns of redwood are illustrated. Solid information for any specifier or user. *California Redwood Association. Price 45¢. Circle No. 500.*

WEATHERVANES. The good old-fashioned copper kind. Many models include horse, rooster, eagle, sulky, goose, cow, deer, pig, arrow, squirrel, whale, fish, sailboat and more. Also included is brochure showing "wee" weathervanes — gazebo size versions of the above. *Ship'N Out, Inc. Circle No. 276.*

THE COLLECTION. Complete line of architectural details from all periods including elaborate cornice mouldings, mantels, rosettes/medallions, niches, overdoor pieces/spandrels, stair brackets, etc. All products are lightweight, factory primed for painting or staining, fire retardant, crisp details, pre-engineered for ease of installation and best of all, affordable. *Focal Point Inc. Price $1.50. Circle No. 419.*

OVERLAID PLYWOOD BETTER THAN PLYWOOD. Ruf-Saw 316 phenolic resin overlaid plywood is available with a wood-grain texture. It takes only half as much paint to cover the overlaid surface and the finish lasts up to three times longer than on raw wood surfaces. *Simpson Timber Co. Price 75¢. Circle No. 422.*

DECORATING WITH CEDAR. A design kit is available to assist the home do-it-yourselfer in the planning and use of decorative cedar shingles. Includes an idea folder showing creative uses for interior and exterior application, graph paper and tracing guide for making to-scale drawings, product information and instructions. *Shakertown Corp. Price $1.00. Circle No. 474.*

HOMEBUYER'S CHECKLIST. A guide to choosing the right home for you and your family. The list contains over 200 items to consider concerning the community, the neighborhood, the lot and the home. Pick out the items critical to you and check them. *General Home Service. Price $2.00. Circle No. 503.*

ENERGY-SAVING PRODUCTS. Literature shows how to find energy-wasting gaps around doors and windows and how to seal them with weatherproofing products. Saving energy reduces fuel bills both in winter and in summer. *Myro, Inc. Circle No. 171.*

MAYTAG ENCYCLOPEDIA OF HOME LAUNDRY. Contains material on energy conservation, fibers, fabric finishes, stain and spot removal and information about home laundry planning and features available on laundry equipment. *Maytag Co. Price $1.25. Circle No. 525.*

RADIO INTERCOM. Unique radio intercommunication systems for homes. Telephone may be answered from any speaker installed in home, garage or patio. Luxury systems to economical packaged radio intercoms provide safety in door answering. *Nutone. Price $1.00. Circle No. 526.*

STAIR-PAK. Finest all-wood spiral stair unit available. Hand-crafted of clear red oak, the spiral fits any decor. It complements wood interiors and provides a pleasing contrast with other interior surfaces. *Stair-Pak Prod. Co. Price 25¢. Circle No. 527.*

REDWOOD SIDING. 4 color brochure offers a variety of handsome richly-toned siding grades and patterns to complete the redwood exterior with a natural complementary touch. Redwood is one of the most durable softwoods, famed for its ability to withstand weather. *Simpson Timber Co. Price 50¢. Circle No. 528.*

FINISHING TOUCH. A booklet for beginners who want to finish or refinish wood. Provides step-by-step instructions for all phases of the wood refinishing process — from removing old paint to the selection and application of new stain and protective finishes. *United Gilsonite Laboratories. Price 25¢. Circle No. 529.*

STATELY COLUMNS & ORNAMENTAL GRILLE WORK. Columns in all sizes, fluted or smooth, round or square, in any length, stand stately and carefree in restoration projects or new construction. Color catalog shows other aluminum products; cast railings, columns, grilles, fences and gates in many elegant designs from the past. *Moultrie Mfg. Co. Price $1.00. Circle No. 542.*

PLANNING A HOME LAUNDRY CENTER. Booklet discusses design, location, storage, work space and possible pitfalls to be avoided. *Maytag Co. Circle No. 247.*

SPIRAL STAIRS. Steel and aluminum model spiral stairs for residence or commercial use. Free-standing stair with quality workmanship. Steel models prefinished dark bronze baked-on enamel. Can be installed in two hours. No special tools required. *Spiral Manufacturing, Inc. Circle No. 173.*

GENUINE LEADED DOOR-LITE INSERTS. Fourteen door styles and numerous glass selections from Visadors Gallery Collection are presented in this 8 page booklet. These door-lite inserts are distinguished by Genuine Hand Leaded and Beveled glass which is mounted in ornately detailed frames. *Visador Co. Price 50¢. Circle No. 524.*

EARTHSTONE, PAVINGSTONE AND ACOUSTICSTONE. Brochures describe these three high quality, cost efficient masonry products which are attractive, strong and an economical means for constructing retaining walls, paved surfaces and noise abatement walls. They cut costs, the need for skilled labor and improve wall aesthetics as well as eliminating the shrinkage and cracking of conventional concrete and earth structures. *Prefab. Circle No. 248.*

ATTIC INSULATION. Literature provides step-by-step instructions for the do-it-yourselfer on how to install fiber glass or rock wool insulation in the attic floor. Everything from how to calculate the proper amount of insulation to how to provide for adequate ventilation is covered. There's even a section on how to hire a contractor if that's preferred. Plus a section on R-values. *Mineral Insulation Manufacturers Association. Price 40¢. Circle No. 499.*

UNDERSTANDING UNDERGROUND WATER. This booklet describes the benefits of individual water systems, discusses types of wells and water system components, and tells how to size a system. *Water Systems Council. Price 45¢. Circle No. 455.*

GOOD CLEAN AIR SWEEPS THE 80'S. Brochures describe the CA/90 Ecologizers, the only products which do the total job of air recirculating, cleaning/deodorizing. *Rush-Hampton Ind. Circle No. 243.*

CATHEDRAL BEAM AND ROOF DECK SYSTEM. Full-color brochure illustrates a collection of decorative beams that are easy to install and will add that touch of distinction to your home. *Laminated Timbers Inc. Circle No. 141.*

WATER FILTER. Literature describes remarkable unit that removes sediment and dirt from all household water. Model VIH installs easily on the main cold water line. Valve is built into the head of the filter. The unit has three modes of operation: on, off and bypass, permitting quick, easy change of cartridges. Fabricated completely of durable, corrosion free, high impact molded plastic. *Filterite Corp. Circle No. 172.*

MICRO-LAM® HEADERS AND BEAMS. A brochure describing MICRO-LAM laminated veneer lumber headers and beams is available from Trus Joist Corp. Stiffer, lighter, longer and stronger than solid sawn lumber, MICRO-LAM® headers and beams will not shrink, warp, split or twist and have been accepted by all major building code authorities. *Trus Joist Corp. Circle No. 204.*

PURE DRINKING WATER. General Ecology's SEAGULL IV residential drinking water purification device is the modern replacement for bottled water. SEAGULL IV removes a wide variety of contaminants including bacteria, TCE, chlorine, and asbestos fibers, making ordinary tap water taste fresh and delicious. Selected for 1982 World's Fair Energy Efficient Home. *General Ecology, Inc. Circle No. 246.*

BEAUTIFUL WOOD FINISHING. 12-page, 4-color "How to Beautifully Finish Wood" booklet enables anyone to create professional finishes the first time with all types of wood. One application of Watco Danish Oil seals, primes, finishes, hardens, protects, beautifies, penetrates deeply into the wood; outlasts surface coats three to one. Nine attractive alcohol-base stain colors also available. *Watco-Dennis Corp. Circle No. 270.*

STAIR KITS. 20-page brochure and price sheet, in easy to understand language, describes spiral stair kits and floating straight stair kits. Factory assistance available for multi-story, special diameters, special layouts, and non-standard floor to floor heights. *The Iron Shop. Circle No. 271.*

ORDER YOUR WATER WELL DONE. A guide to locating and constructing water wells. Water quality control is also discussed. *Water Systems Council. Price 75¢. Circle No. 454.*

RAIL-PAK. Made entirely of clear red oak and styled for a clean, contemporary look, RAIL-PAK is a pre-assembled rail system requiring minimum effort and tools to install. *Stair-Pak Prod. Co. Circle No. 272.*

CHIMNEY FLUE CAP. All metal welded construction. Keeps out rain and snow, preventing rust damage to dampers. Keeps in sparks and cinders. Stops birds and squirrels from entering chimney. Stops leaves and other debris from collecting in the flue. *Hutch Mfg. Circle No. 273.*

RESIDENTIAL SPRINKLER KIT. The first U.L. listed residential sprinkler, Grinnell's Model F954 to enhance life safety is available at $10.00 each. White frame arm or brass finish. Residential fire sprinkler kits include all devices (except piping and hangers) necessary to satisfy requirements of N.F.P.A. Standard 13D available at price of $498. Send for catalog sheet. *Grinnell Fire Protection. Circle No. 274.*

STAIR LOCK. Literature describes a stairway system called "Stair Lock" which features pre-machined interlocking parts which can be assembled and installed in one hour, with no technical skill required. Reversible parts create a variable rise and run that is designed to fit most of today's homes. *Visador Co. 35¢. Circle No. 501.*

MONEY SAVERS. Products designed to help you save on water, sewer and energy bills and to conserve energy. *Ecology Prod. Plus, Inc. Circle No. 249.*

ENERGY SAVING MONEY SAVING ITEMS. Tabloid tells of energy saving products designed to cut down on high utility bills. Everything from air deflectors, water heater blankets, to insulation. *Deflect-o Corporation. Circle No. 245.*

WOODMASTER IS A WALL . . . A woodmaster space divider is your key to getting more efficient use from any interior space. Create an extra bedroom or private den at a moment's notice. Colorful brochure describes how. *Modernfold. Circle No. 119.*

Literature order form

Order the Information You Want Today . . .

STEP I. Circle the numbers corresponding to the literature in this publication that you want. Please enclose $1.50 processing fee.

FREE BROCHURES & CATALOGS:

101	102	104	107	108	109	110	113
114	116	118	119	121	122	125	126
127	128	133	137	138	139	141	143
145	146	149	151	152	154	156	160
161	162	164	167	169	171	172	173
177	181	182	185	188	189	191	192
194	195	196	204	208	209	210	213
216	218	224	225	227	228	229	231
232	234	235	236	239	240	241	242
243	245	246	247	248	249	250	253
254	255	256	257	258	259	260	261
262	263	264	265	266	267	268	269
270	271	272	273	274	275	276	277
278	279	280	281				

PRICED LITERATURE:

403 25¢	408 50¢	409 75¢	410 25¢	418 $3	419 $1.50
420 75¢	422 75¢	428 $1	429 $1	431 $1	433 25¢
435 25¢	440 30¢	443 50¢	444 $1	445 $3	446 $1
447 $1	448 10¢	449 10¢	450 25¢	451 35¢	454 75¢
455 45¢	456 25¢	460 $1	465 50¢	466 50¢	474 $1
475 50¢	476 $1	484 50¢	486 25¢	491 40¢	492 25¢
493 15¢	495 $2	498 35¢	499 40¢	500 45¢	501 35¢
502 50¢	503 $2	504 $3	505 $19.50	508 50¢	509 $3.50
510 $2.50	511 $1	512 $1	513 50¢	515 10¢	516 $1
517 $2.50	518 75¢	519 $2	520 $1	521 25¢	522 50¢
523 75¢	524 50¢	525 $1.25	526 $1	527 25¢	528 50¢
529 25¢	530 $3.50	531 $3.50	532 $1	533 75¢	534 50¢
535 $4	536 50¢	537 $5	538 $3.50	539 $3.50	540 50¢
541 $5	542 $1	543 25¢			

Complete Order Form Next Page . . .

Come home to quality.
Come home to Andersen.™

Free window info!

Here's *the* window and gliding patio door booklet for new homes, remodeling and window replacing. 24 pages of facts and figures in easy to understand question and answer format. You'll also find beautiful full-color photos for window ideas and special sections on energy and window planning. The complete Andersen line (with size tables) is shown installed in homes. Mail coupon to Andersen Corp., Box 12, Bayport, Minnesota 55003.

Name_____

Address_____

City_____ State_____

Zip_____ Phone(___)_____
Area Code

Andersen Windowalls®
ANDERSEN CORPORATION   BAYPORT, MINNESOTA 55003

123-0682

Literature order form/continued

STEP II. Please help us out by answering these questions:

1. Are you:
- ☐ Building a new home
- ☐ Buying a new home
- ☐ Buying an older home
- ☐ Remodeling your present home

2. If you are building a new home . . .

   A. Are you planning to start construction within the next six months?   ☐ yes ☐ no

   B. Do you presently own the land that you plan to build on?   ☐ yes ☐ no

   C. How will your home be built?
- ☐ Through a general building contractor
- ☐ With you acting as general contractor
- ☐ With you doing most of the actual labor

   D. Where are you getting the construction drawings for your new home?
- ☐ Garlinghouse or another home plans company
- ☐ Architect or local designer
- ☐ Provided by your building contractor
- ☐ Other _____

3. A. Which best describes the size of the closest community or population center to where you live:
- ☐ Under 10,000 population
- ☐ 100,000 to 500,000 population
- ☐ 10,000 to 50,000 population
- ☐ 500,000 to 1,000,000 population
- ☐ 50,000 to 100,000 population
- ☐ over 1,000,000 population

   B. Do you live:
- ☐ Within the above community or in its immediate suburb
- ☐ In a rural area, some distance from the above community

4. What is your approximate age?
- ☐ 18-24
- ☐ 50-64
- ☐ 25-34
- ☐ 65 or older
- ☐ 35-49

5. What is the age of your youngest child living at home?
- ☐ No children at home
- ☐ 10-18 years
- ☐ Under 3 years
- ☐ over 18 years
- ☐ 3-9 years

6. What products do you plan to have in your new home?
- ☐ Insulated (double or triple paned) windows and glass door
- ☐ Fireplace and/or wood burning stove
- ☐ Automatic garage door opener
- ☐ Central Air Conditioning
- ☐ Skylights
- ☐ Microwave Oven
- ☐ Dishwasher
- ☐ Washer and Dryer
- ☐ Heat Pump
- ☐ Wall Paneling

7. Are you or a member of your family professionally involved in the building field? If so, please indicate how:
- ☐ No involvement
- ☐ Building contractor
- ☐ Building sub-contractor
- ☐ Architect
- ☐ Home designer (other than architect)
- ☐ Lumber dealer
- ☐ Other building material supplier
- ☐ Engineer involved in residential housing
- ☐ Other _____
- _____

Step III.

GHPG-4

Fill in your proper mailing address:

Name _____

Address _____

City _____

State _____ Zip _____

Step IV.

Figure the amount due and enclose a check or money order

Amount due for priced literature $ _____

Processing Fee $ ___1.50___

Kansas Residents Add 3½% Sales Tax $ _____

TOTAL AMOUNT ENCLOSED $ _____

Allow 3-6 weeks for delivery.

Step V. Make checks payable and mail complete page to:

The Product Information Source

P.O. Box 1735, Topeka, Kansas 66601-1735

ONLY PRODUCT LITERATURE MAY BE ORDERED FROM THIS ADDRESS. TO ORDER BLUEPRINTS SEE PAGES 108-109. TO ORDER BUILDING BOOKS SEE PAGE 112.

Underground Home Cuts Energy Use

No. 10364—Oriented to a southern exposure, this underground home combines all the comforts of a well-planned contemporary with a fraction of the typical energy consumption. The pre-stressed concrete roof is covered with two feet of earth, a highly effective insulator, to keep winter cold out, warmth in. Walls on three sides are of 8-inch poured concrete. In addition to its functional approach, the plan is highly livable . . . with a protected patio reached by sliding glass doors and an immense open living area featuring family room, living room, and kitchen with snack bar. Bedrooms are large, and the master bedroom annexes a private bath and three closets. A utility/laundry room, double garage and chimneys for gas furnace and wood stove are included.

House—1,795 sq. ft., Garage—576 sq. ft.

For price and order information see pages 108-109

BEDROOM
12'-8"X15'-0"

BEDROOM
15'-6"X10'-9"

UTILITY RM.
15'-6"X 7'-1"

KITCHEN
11'-0"X11'-4"

FAMILY ROOM
16'-0" X 15'-6"

MASTER BEDROOM
12'-8"X15'-3"

PATIO

LIVING ROOM
15'-0" X15'-9"

GARAGE
23'-4"X23'-0"

72'-8"

48'-0"

50'-0"

TERRACE

NO. 10364

DRIVEWAY

Double decks benefit two story

No. 10278—Serving first floor kitchen and dining room and two second floor bedrooms, the double decks become practical and appealing elements in this angular contemporary. Living areas zone themselves by extending in three directions on the first level, and bedrooms maintain privacy in the same way on the level above. Besides the half bath bordering the utility room, the design shows two full baths, one with a dressing area off the master bedroom. A snack bar is featured in the kitchen.

First floor—904 sq. ft., Second floor—768 sq. ft.

Foyer creates efficient traffic pattern

No. 1030—Bedrooms, living room, and family-kitchen are easily accessible from the long entrance foyer of this brick-sheathed traditional. At right, the living room spans over 19 feet and connects to the kitchen for entertaining ease. Open to the patio via sliding glass doors, the family room-kitchen complex becomes an informal activity center, complete with snack bar, laundry niche, and broom closet. The sleeping zone is comprised of four bedrooms and two full baths.

First floor—1,494 sq. ft., Garage—522 sq. ft.

Plan offers first floor laundry, shop

No. 10188—Natural wood shapes the exterior of this contemporary design, arranged for living and working. Off the garage, a functional shop provides a haven for the hobbyist, while the utility room houses laundry equipment for step-saving efficiency. Plentiful expanses of glass bathe the home in natural light, and storage space is abundant. Radiating from the well-planned compartmented bath, three bedrooms fill the upper level. Another half bath is featured below, equally convenient to living and family rooms.

First floor—1,110 sq. ft., Second floor—683 sq. ft.
Garage and shop—657 sq. ft.

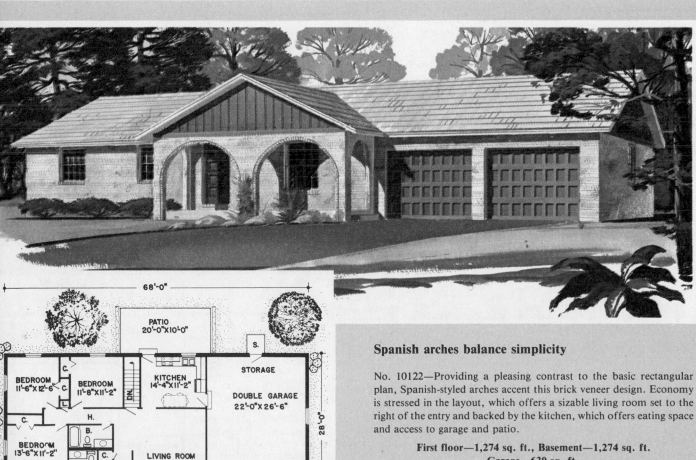

Spanish arches balance simplicity

No. 10122—Providing a pleasing contrast to the basic rectangular plan, Spanish-styled arches accent this brick veneer design. Economy is stressed in the layout, which offers a sizable living room set to the right of the entry and backed by the kitchen, which offers eating space and access to garage and patio.

First floor—1,274 sq. ft., Basement—1,274 sq. ft.
Garage—630 sq. ft.

*For price and order information
see pages 108-109*

Rectangle shapes winning design

No. 214—Sharp and simple, this rectangular ranch style frames four bedrooms, two baths, and open, enjoyable living area. Tiled entry with coat closet flows into the living-dining area, where a crackling fireplace sets the stage for relaxing conversation and pleasurable dining. The area is open to the functional kitchen and, via sliding glass doors, to the terrace. Two sinks equip the main bath, while the double-closeted master bedroom luxuriates in a bath with shower. An extra large double garage grants additional storage space.

First floor—1,484 sq. ft., Basement—1,092 sq. ft.
Garage—480 sq. ft.

Sliding glass doors open to the terrace

No. 218—Families with small children will appreciate the artfully outlined floor plan in this economical brick trimmed ranch style. Two full baths serve the bedroom wing, and the larger of the two is assigned to the parents' bedroom. Laundry space is located near the main bath, and a storage closet, perfect for toys and games, edges the hallway. Sliding glass doors in the living room open to the terrace, a logical play area visible from most rooms of the home. Another asset is the front entry with coat closet.

First floor—1,245 sq. ft., Garage—464 sq. ft., Storage—70 sq. ft.

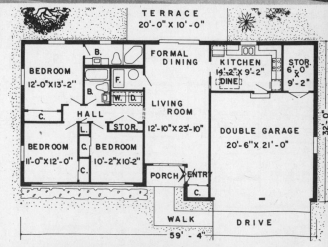

Living room expresses warmth, formality

No. 10088—Set to the left of the tiled foyer and adjoining a formal dining room, the living room of this trim ranch style offers an expansive area for entertaining and relaxing before a warm wood fire. Connected to the dining room via sliding glass doors is a large dining porch that encourages cookouts and informal parties. Family activity is centered in the kitchen/family room, with sliding glass doors connecting it to the rear patio. Three bedrooms include a luxurious master bedroom with walk-in closet and private bath.

First floor—1,655 sq. ft., Basement—1,655 sq. ft.
Garage—535 sq. ft.

For price and order information
see pages 108-109

Mansard roof caps compact home

No. 10084—Modest in square footage, this mansard roof design provides an up-to-date, appealing home for a small family or retired couple. Entry is into the spacious living room, with coat closet at left, and placement of kitchen and dining area beyond results in a minimum of wasted space. Plentiful closet space is a plus, and the master bedroom is favored with two, including a large walk-in closet. Handy to bedrooms and bath is the hall laundry niche, and for relaxing, the dining area merits sliding glass doors to the patio.

First floor—1,053 sq. ft., Basement—1,053 sq. ft.
Garage and storage—373 sq. ft.

101

Shake shingles layer rustic traditional

No. 258—Shuttered dormer windows and brick chimney augment the rustic shake shingles in welding a singular exterior for this two-story traditional. Inside, rooms are fairly sizable and storage space abundant. Living room is placed to the left of the entry and enjoys a fireplace, while dining room borders the kitchen on the right. Two bedrooms upstairs supplement the small bedroom or den with half bath on main level. A spacious full bath is featured upstairs, and double closets furnish each bedroom.

First floor—852 sq. ft., Second floor—570 sq. ft.
Basement—852 sq. ft.

Kitchen functional, multi-purpose

No. 220—Favored with breakfast bar and laundry center, the kitchen in this brick and stone-trimmed plan functions efficiently and is placed to serve both family room and living room. Family room's warm log-burning fireplace creates an unmatched atmosphere that drifts into the kitchen as well, while the living room sets aside an area for formal entertaining. Useful closets line the three bedrooms, which include a generously-proportioned master bedroom meriting bath with shower.

First floor—1,548 sq. ft., Basement—1,387 sq. ft.
Garage—321 sq. ft.

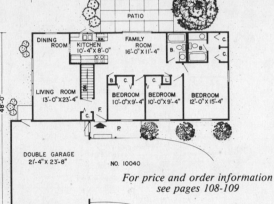

Moderate traditional filled with space

No. 10040—Incorporating family room, extensive living room and elegant master bedroom, this design provides a well-planned, comfortable home in only 1296 square feet of living space. Exterior is traditional and blends small-paned windows, shutters and cupola. Floor plan shows living and family rooms connected by a corridor kitchen, and both rooms are accessible from the foyer. Open to the family room through sliding glass doors, the terrace extends living areas.

First floor—1,296 sq. ft., Basement—1,296 sq. ft. Garage—528 sq. ft.

For price and order information see pages 108-109

Sun deck crowns rustic exterior

No. 9978—Rough cedar plywood battened siding joined with a shake shingle mansard roof radiate a rusticity that is appropriately topped with a large sun deck over the garage. Befitting either a lakeshore, mountain or urban lot, this three bedroom home also details a ground level terrace with staircase spiraling upward to the sun deck. The family room opens to both garage and terrace, and the formal living room looks out on the shaded front porch.

First floor—1,176 sq. ft., Basement—1,176 sq. ft. Garage—572 sq. ft.

Terrace dining possibility in plan

No. 394—Sliding glass doors open the dining area to the terrace of this trim, brick-veneer plan and suggest relaxed outdoor dining. Only steps from the terrace, the kitchen emphasizes efficiency and boasts center work island, laundry niche, and garage entrance. Serving as focal point of the design is the comfortable living room, with bedrooms clustered to the left. Master bedroom merits half bath and walk-in closet. An extra-long double garage offers plentiful storage space and three entrances.

First floor—1,244 sq. ft., Garage—466 sq. ft.

Cozy plan stresses family living

No. 398—Covering only 1,043 square feet of living space, this compact design maximizes space for family activities. the comfortably large living room is backed by a well-planned family room open to the kitchen and featuring a handy garage entrance. Sliding glass doors enlarge the family room to the terrace, which promises outdoor barbecues and a natural setting for children's play. Two bedrooms are equally convenient to the full bath, and storage areas are outlined for garage and kitchen.

First floor—1,043 sq. ft., Garage—458 sq. ft.

Charm, practicality blend in plan

No. 1006—Imposing columns and shuttered small-paned windows paint a picturesque facade for this three bedroom traditional. Inside and out, the plan fuses charm with convenience to produce covered patio, tiled foyer, and cozy family room.

**First floor—1,300 sq. ft., Carport—400 sq. ft.
Exterior storage—60 sq. ft.**

Hillside lot suits family layout

No. 10074—Planned for a hillside lot, this contemporary home offers three bedrooms plus a convenient nursery to accommodate a growing family. Entry is across the roofed porch and into the well-windowed living room. Bordering kitchen spans over 18 feet to provide space for laundry equipment and a large pantry.

**First floor—1,624 sq. ft., Basement—1,104 sq. ft.
Garage—520 sq. ft.**

*For price and order information
see pages 108-109*

Have a hobby and the room

No. 10014—This three bedroom Ranch design will be economical to build and easy to maintain. The hipped roof eliminates all gable ends, eliminating that painting problem. The brick veneer adds esthetic value and requires very little care. The floor plan features an excellent traffic pattern. Notice how all bathroom and laundry plumbing is grouped together for maximum installation economy. There is a hobby room behind the garage.

First floor—1,383 sq. ft., Hobby room—238 sq. ft. Garage—485 sq. ft.

Rugged materials give ranch house effect

No. 9842—The textured exterior materials and exposed rafter ends give this home a rugged ranch house appearance. A small front porch, back screened-in porch and large terrace are designed for the family who likes to live in-and-out-of-doors. The kitchen, opening onto the family room, contains built-in range, oven, dishwasher, desk and broom closet. The foyer channels traffic to the three bedrooms, the family room or the living room with its own built-in fireplace. A double garage and full basement provide storage and room for recreation.

First floor—1,435 sq. ft., Basement—1,360 sq. ft. Garage—545 sq. ft.

Double sliding glass doors join terrace

No. 10042—Joining the terrace with living-dining room, two sets of sliding glass doors admit light and involve indoors with outdoors in this L-shaped traditional. Tiled foyer steers traffic to all areas, and separate bedroom zone boasts a full bath shared by master bedroom and family room for maximum efficiency. Storage space lines one wall of the double garage, and full basement provides additional storage, laundry, and recreation areas.

First floor—1,302 sq. ft., Basement—1,302 sq. ft.
Garage—594 sq. ft.

Basement can be added

No. 9952—A sunken living room, wood burning fireplace, flagstone terrace, large sun deck with spiral stairway, four bedrooms, and a unique exterior are some of the desirable features of this attractive home. The drawings show basementless construction, however, an alternative plan shows how a basement stairway can be included. The half bath near the rear entrance will serve as a mud room. The front center bedroom will make an excellent office if needed.

First floor—1,619 sq. ft., Garage—612 sq. ft.

For price and order information see pages 108-109

GARLINGHOUSE

ORDER YOUR NE
From a compa

ANOTHER GARLINGHOUSE DESIGN

- Experience the thrill of creating and customizing your home.
- Enjoy comparing and choosing options.
- Obtain construction bids . . . and you're ready to build.

For 75 years, Garlinghouse homes have been built by tens of thousands o families across the nation. The construction blueprints are complete . . . accurate . . . and contain all the information a builder needs to begin construction.

GARLINGHOUSE PLANS SAVE YOU MONEY

The costs of designing our homes are spread over a number of plan buyers nationwide. Therefore, you pay only a fraction of what you would spend to have a home designed (specifically for you).

BLUEPRINT MODIFICATIONS

It is expensive to have plans modified by professional designers. However minor alterations in design, as well as building material substitutions, can be made by any competent builder according to the needs or wishes of the home owners.

YOU CAN CHARGE YOUR ORDER!

TO ORDER PRODUCT LITERATURE SEE PAGES 95-9

BLUEPRINT ORDER FORM

PLEASE SEND ME:
- ☐ One Complete Set of Blueprints
- ☐ Minimum Construction Package five sets
- ☐ Standard Construction Package eight sets

Plan Number _____ ☐ as shown ☐ reversed

Cost . . . .$_____

_____ **Additional Set(s)** $15.00 each . . . .$_____

Materials List ($10.00 per order) . . . .$_____

Mailing Charges . . . .$____4.25____

TOTAL AMOUNT ENCLOSED . . . .$_____
(Kansas residents add 3 1/2%)

CHARGE MY ORDER TO:
☐ Mastercharge ☐ Visa ☐ American Express

Exp.
Card # _____ Date _____

Signature _____

WE WOULD APPRECIATE YOUR HELP IN ANSWERING THE FOLLOWING QUESTIONS:

	Yes	No
Do you now own the land you plan to build on?	☐	☐
Do you plan to start construction in the next 6 months?	☐	☐
Do you plan to build most of the home yourself?	☐	☐
Would you like for us to have free building product information sent to you?	☐	☐

Name _____

Address _____

City_____ State_____ Zip_____

The Garlinghouse Co., 320 S.W. 33rd St., P.O. Box 299
(913) 267-2490   Topeka, Kansas 66601-0299

BLUEPRINT ORDER FORM

PLEASE SEND ME:
- ☐ One Complete Set of Blueprints
- ☐ Minimum Construction Package five sets
- ☐ Standard Construction Package eight sets

Plan Number _____ ☐ as shown ☐ revers

Cost . . . .$_____

_____ **Additional Set(s)** $15.00 each . . . .$_____

Materials List ($10.00 per order) . . . .$_____

Mailing Charges . . . .$____4.25____

TOTAL AMOUNT ENCLOSED . . . .$_____
(Kansas residents add 3 1/2%)

CHARGE MY ORDER TO:
☐ Mastercharge ☐ Visa ☐ American Express

Exp.
Card # _____ Date ____

Signature _____

WE WOULD APPRECIATE YOUR HELP IN ANSWERING THE FOLLOWING QUESTIONS:

	Yes	
Do you now own the land you plan to build on?	☐	
Do you plan to start construction in the next 6 months?	☐	
Do you plan to build most of the home yourself?	☐	
Would you like for us to have free building product information sent to you?	☐	

Name _____

Address _____

City_____ State_____ Zip_____

The Garlinghouse Co., 320 S.W. 33rd St., P.O. Box 299
(913) 267-2490   Topeka, Kansas 66601-0299

HOME BLUEPRINTS ... TODAY!!
ith 75 years of experience.

WHAT IS INCLUDED IN A SET OF GARLINGHOUSE BLUEPRINTS?

1) Four Elevations (Views of the Outside)
2) Floor Plans (1/4" to 1' scale) for all floors
3) Basement and/or Foundation Plan
4) Roof Plan
5) Typical Wall Sections
6) Kitchen and Bath Cabinet Details
7) Fireplace Detail (where applicable)
8) Detail for Stairs (where applicable)
9) Plot Plan
10) Electrical Layout
11) Complete Materials List (if Ordered)
12) Specifications & Contract Form

REVERSE PLANS

You may find that a particular house would suit you or your lot condition better if it were reversed. A reverse plan turns the design end for end. That is, if the garage is shown on the left side and the bedrooms on the right, the reverse plan will show the garage on the right side and the bedrooms on the left. To see how a design will look in reverse, hold the book in front of a mirror. Dimensions and lettering of most Garlinghouse reverse plans are right reading. When this is not the case, one mirror image set is produced for reference by you and your builder, and the rest are sent "as shown" for ease of reading lettering and dimensions. (Available only on multiple set orders.)

MONEY BACK GUARANTEE

All Garlinghouse Blueprints are sold with a ten day unconditional money back guarantee. Study the plan sets for ten days ... even get an opinion from your builder. If you are not completely satisfied, then return the blueprints and your money will be cheerfully refunded ... no questions asked.

INTERNATIONAL ORDERS

If you are ordering from outside the United States, then your check, money order, or international money transfer should be payable in U.S. currency. Because of the extremely long delays involved with surface mail, we ship all orders from outside the U.S.A., Canada or Mexico via Air Mail. There is a total mailing charge of $22.00 on these orders.

Canadian and Mexican orders are normally shipped by first class mail. Please include $7.00 for mailing charges on these orders. If you wish to have your order shipped into Mexico via Air Mail, then you will need to enclose $9.00 to cover the mailing charges.

All blueprints orders are shipped UPS or Priority Mail (usually on the same day the order is received.

An additional flat charge of $10.00 is required to have a materials list included with each set of plans ordered.

Prices are subject to change without notice.

PRICE SCHEDULE

SINGLE FAMILY HOMES	1 set	5 sets	8 sets
Under 1400 sq. ft.	$60.00	$ 95.00	$120.00
1400 to 2400 sq. ft.	65.00	100.00	125.00
Over 2400 sq. ft.	70.00	105.00	130.00

Additional sets $15.00 each. — Materials list $10.00 per order.

BLUEPRINT ORDER FORM

PLEASE SEND ME:
- ☐ One Complete Set of Blueprints
- ☐ Minimum Construction Package five sets
- ☐ Standard Construction Package eight sets

Plan Number _____ ☐ as shown ☐ reversed

Cost . . . . $_____

_____ Additional Set(s) $15.00 each. . . . . . . $_____

Materials List ($10.00 per order) . . . . $_____

Mailing Charges . . . . $____ 4.25

TOTAL AMOUNT ENCLOSED . . . . $_____
(Kansas residents add 3 1/2%)

CHARGE MY ORDER TO:
- ☐ Mastercharge ☐ Visa ☐ American Express
  Exp.
Card # _____ Date _____

Signature _____

WE WOULD APPRECIATE YOUR HELP IN ANSWERING THE FOLLOWING QUESTIONS:

	Yes	No
Do you now own the land you plan to build on?	☐	☐
Do you plan to start construction in the next 6 months?	☐	☐
Do you plan to build most of the home yourself?	☐	☐
Would you like for us to have free building product information sent to you?	☐	☐

Name _____

Address _____

City _____ State _____ Zip _____

**The Garlinghouse Co., 320 S.W. 33rd St., P.O. Box 299
(913) 267-2490   Topeka, Kansas 66601-0299**

FREE ENERGY CONSERVATION SPECIFICATION GUIDE

Let Us Help You Save Dollars In Fuel Costs!

We don't need to tell you about high energy costs — you already know that . . .

But did you know that many peoples fuel bills equal or exceed their house payment? Or that fuel prices are expected to TRIPLE within the next ten years?

At Garlinghouse, we care, and we want to help you save those fuel dollars in your new home! In fact, we feel this is so important, that we have prepared a new **Energy Conservation Specification Guide** for our customers. And it's FREE with every blueprint order!

Here in one complete easy-to understand guide learn:
- About 22 fuel-saving measures **you** can use!
- How home location affects fuel costs.
- About the different types of insulation available and what they can do for you.
- How a few details can go a long way in saving energy.
- How, with the aid of our insulation spec. charts to plan your insulation needs.

It's all yours — FREE

109

Building Books

**ORDER FORM
PAGE 112**

The books on this page were written with the professional home builder in mind. They are all comprehensive information sources for contractors or for those beginners who wish to build like contractors.

2546. Blueprint Reading For Construction This combination text and workbook shows and tells how to read residential, commercial, and light industrial prints. With an abundance of actual drawings from industry, you learn step by step about each component of a set of blueprints, including even cost estimating. 336 pp.; Goodheart-Willcox (spiral bound) **$23.00**

2556. Handbook of Doormaking, Windowmaking, and Staircasing This publication is dedicated to the presentation of an almost lost art: Quality workmanship in homebuilding! This completely illustrated handbook offers clear, step-by-step instructions that will allow any carpenter (amateur or professional) to construct finely crafted doors, windows and staircases. This book is meant for those who wish to take the time to build a quality home that will last. 256 pp.; 377 illus. Sterling Publishing (paperback) **$7.95**

2570. Modern Masonry Everything you will ever need to know about concrete, masonry and brick is included in this book. Forms construction, concrete reinforcement, proper foundation construction, and bricklaying are among the topics covered in step-by-step detail. An excellent all-round reference and guide. 256 pp.; 700 illus. Goodheart-Willcox **$12.80**

2504. Architecture, Residential Drawing and Design An excellent text that explains all the fundamentals on how to create a complete set of construction drawings. Specific areas covered include proper design and planning considerations, foundation plans, floor plans, elevations, stairway details, electrical plans, plumbing plans, etc. 492 pp.; over 800 illus. Goodheart-Willcox **$25.60**

2508. Modern Plumbing All aspects of plumbing installation, service, and repair are presented here in illustrated, easy-to-follow text. This book contains all the information needed for vocational competence, including the most up-to-date tools, materials, and practices. 300 pp.; over 700 illus. Goodheart-Willcox **$14.00**

2506. House Wiring Simplified This book teaches all the fundamentals of modern house wiring; shows how it's done with easy-to-understand drawings. A thorough guide to the materials and practices for safe, efficient installation of home electrical systems. 176 pp.; 384 illus. Goodheart-Willcox **$8.00**

2510. Modern Carpentry A complete guide to the "nuts and bolts" of building a home. This book explains all about building materials, framing, trim work, insulation, foundations, and much more. A valuable text and reference guide. 492 pp.; over 1400 illus. Goodheart-Willcox **$14.00**

2544. Solar Houses An examination of solar homes from the standpoint of lifestyle. This publication shows you through photographs, interviews, and practical information, what a solar lifestyle involves, how owners react to it, and what the bottom-line economics are. Included are 130 floor plans and diagrams which give you a clear idea of how various "active" and "passive" solar systems work. 160 pp.; 370 illus. Pantheon (paperback) **$9.95**

2558. Build Your Own Stone House A practical guide to stone house construction using the unique "Slipform Method" that saves time and effort. In this photo filled book, crammed with charts, tables, diagrams, and sketches, you learn all the essentials for building a stone house, including a thorough discussion of materials, siting, excavation, making and using slipforms, fireplaces, etc. An exciting breakthrough in stone house construction. 156 pp.; Garden Way (paperback) **$6.95**

2536. Build Your Own Solar Water Heater A nuts and bolts guide written in clear "how-to-do-it" terms. This book describes only workable, efficient systems that can be built with off-the-shelf plumbing components. Also included is a complete discussion of collectors, financial analysis of solar hot water systems, and even special considerations for solar heated swimming pool systems. 120 pp.; 75 illus. Garden Way (paperback) **$8.95**

2518. Build Your Own Home An authoritative guide on how to be your own general contractor. This book goes through the step-by-step process of building a house with special emphasis on the business aspects such as financing, scheduling, permits, insurance, and more. Furthermore, it gives you an understanding of what to expect out of your various subcontractors so that you can properly orchestrate their work. 106 pp.; Holland House (paperback) **$8.95**

2554. Underground Houses A fabulously detailed account of the actual building process for an underground home. This book follows the author through the step-by-step construction of his 910 square foot energy efficient, sub-grade dwelling (which incidentally cost only $6,750 to build). If you are interested in building an underground home with your own two hands and you want to build it right the first time, then you will want to have this well illustrated, easy to follow guide. 128 pp.; Sterling (paperback) **$5.95**

2552. Cordwood Masonry Houses: A Practical Guide for the Owner-Builder This book provides the knowledge by which anyone can build a "dream home" for minimal cost (as little as $5.00 per square foot). Cordwood masonry is an age-old method of construction that utilizes very short logs laid up like firewood with mortar fill between them. This practical guide explains exactly how to construct an energy efficient cordwood masonry home that will last almost forever. It is supplemented with case histories which include color photos. An excellent book for the home builder who is not afraid to use unconventional building materials. 168 pp; Sterling Publishing (paperback) **$7.95**

2564. Landscaping Design That Saves Energy This book is a practical and attractive guide to landscaping techniques that can reduce your heating and cooling needs by as much as 30%. Careful landscaping design can modify wind, solar radiation, and precipitation and can temper extremes of climate. This book contains specific planting strategies for the four major climatic zones of the continental U.S. It is an excellent reference for creating an effective low-cost landscaping plan that will keep appreciating the value of your home year after year, at the same time it is becoming more beautiful and effective in saving energy. 219 pp.; Morrow Quill Paperbacks (paperback) **$9.95**

2560. The House Book How livable your new home turns out to be is determined primarily by the interior finishing and decorating that goes into your home. This book is the bible of home decorating, covering absolutely every aspect of interior finishing. It contains over 1000 color photographs with a wealth of ideas new to the U.S. (European decors). This is the most comprehensive and informative book on home decorating that you can buy. It's well worth the investment. 448 pp.; Crown (paperback) **$14.95**

2566. Solar Dwelling Designs The focus of this well illustrated publication is how the interaction of climate, comfort, building sites and solar systems influence the design of solar heated and cooled dwellings. It contains a thorough discussion of the theory and actual operation of various solar systems, all in easy to understand, non-technical language. Also covered in detail are the specifics of various solar dwelling designs. 144 pp.; Sterling (paperback) **$5.95**

2514. The Underground House Book For anyone seriously interested in building and living in an underground home, this book tells it all. Aesthetic considerations, building codes, site planning, financing, insurance, planning and decorating considerations, maintenance costs, soil, excavation, landscaping, water considerations, humidity control, and specific case histories are among the many facets of underground living dealt with in this publication. 208 pp.; 140 illus. Garden Way **$10.95**

2562. How To Design and Build Your Own House Illustrated with almost 700 drawings (every step of the way), this complete do-it-yourself manual enables you, the beginner, to design and construct your own house. From putting together your first ideas and translating them into working drawings to figuring out costs and the actual construction of the house. The most complete and best illustrated book on the subject. 384 pp.; Alfred A. Knopf (paperback) **$10.95**

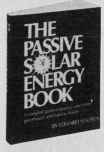

2540. The Passive Solar Energy Book A surprisingly complete guide to passive solar home, greenhouse, and building design. This book presents a step-by-step process for choosing and sizing the systems best suited for your particular needs. Includes information about solar radiation, regional climate variations, and space heat losses and gains so that you can calculate heating/cooling requirements and determine the potential money savings with a passive solar system. 448 pp.; 238 illus. Rodale (paperback) **$14.95**

Building Books Order Form

PLEASE SEND ME THE FOLLOWING BOOKS:

Book Order Number	Price
_____	$ _____
_____	$ _____
_____	$ _____
_____	$ _____
_____	$ _____
Postage and Handling	$ ____1.75____
Add 50¢ For Each Additional Book	$ _____
Kansas Residents Add 3½% Sales Tax	$ _____
TOTAL ENCLOSED	**$** _____

- Orders usually shipped the same day they are received
- International Orders include an additional $1.50 per book for surface mail

CHARGE MY ORDER TO:

☐ **MasterCard**　　☐ **Visa**　　☐ **American Express**

Card # _____　Exp. Date _____

Signature _____

_____

MY SHIPPING ADDRESS IS:
(Please Print)

Name _____

Address _____

City _____

State _____ Zip _____

05056

SEND ORDER TO:
The Garlinghouse Company
P.O. Box 299
Topeka, Kansas 66601-0299

Prices subject to change without notice.

112

2532. Harnessing The Wind For Home Energy Windpower! Is it for you? This book includes an in-depth analysis assessing the potential of your home site for using wind energy; the various types of systems available and which is best for you; return or payback on investment; and a listing of manufacturers of wind power systems. If you have ever considered using wind energy, then this is the book for you. 144 pp.; Garden Way (paperback) **$6.95**

2650. Multi-level Hillside & Solar Home Plans
2651. Single-level & Underground Home Plans
2652. Traditional Home Plans
Each of these three books contain over 120 new, innovative home designs from the finest architects and designers all over America. Many full color illustrations, and blueprints are available for all homes. 116pp.; Garlinghouse (paperback) Each **$2.50**

2516. Building Consultant The new home buyer's bible to home construction. This encyclopedia of home building explains in comprehensive detail about all the various elements that go into a completed house. It enables you to deal with the construction of your new home in a meaningful way that will avoid costly errors, whether you use a contractor or build it yourself. 188 pp.; Holland House (paperback) **$8.95**

2542. Designing and Building A Solar House Written by one of America's foremost authorities on solar architecture. It is a practical "how-to" guide that clearly demonstrates the most sensible ways to marry good house design with contemporary solar technology. Included is a thorough discussion of both "active" and "passive" solar systems, and even a listing of the today's leading solar homes. 288 pp.; 400 illus. Garden Way (paperback) **$10.95**

2550. The Complete Book of Woodburning Stoves Here is an all-encompassing guide to the stoves currently available on the market, including coverage of the components necessary for proper operation of woodburning stoves (such as chimneys, flues, etc.), and the various grades of fuel which should be used for top efficiency. A listing of wood stove manufacturers makes this book particularly useful to anyone who wants to heat their home with wood. 160 pp.; Sterling (paperback) **$6.95**

2522. How To Build Your Own Home For the person who wants to build a home with his own two hands. This publication explains in generously illustrated detail, each step of the construction process, leaving nothing out. Surveying, excavating, carpentry, plumbing, heating, and resilient flooring are just a few of the many items covered. 356 pp.; Structures (paperback) **$9.95**